WOMEN PASTORS AND GOD'S ORDAINED ORDER

LOUIS R. TORRES

TEACH Services, Inc.
P U B L I S H I N G
www.TEACHServices.com • (800) 367-1844

Copyright © 2022 Louis R. Torres
Copyright © 2022 TEACH Services, Inc.
ISBN-13: 978-1-4796-1516-2 (Paperback)
ISBN-13: 978-1-4796-1517-9 (ePub)
Library of Congress Control Number: 2022906263

All scripture references are taken from the King James Version (KJV) of the Bible. Public domain.

Published by

TEACH Services, Inc.
P U B L I S H I N G
www.TEACHServices.com • (800) 367-1844

Table of Contents

1

Equally Different

I was riding in a New York City subway train about midday. As my eyes scanned the different overhead advertisements, my attention was arrested by a poster. It was a sequence of three pictures. The first was of a man sitting against the trunk of a large acorn tree casting its umbrella-like cooling shade over him. Just in front of the man, in the second picture, was an index-finger-thick vine bearing enormous heavy pumpkins. Underneath, there was a caption that read: "How foolish of God to place such a large pumpkin on a tiny vine and such small nuts on a large tree." The third picture was of an acorn landing on his head with a caption that read: "Man thinks himself wise until God shows him his folly." Immediately, he saw God's wisdom.

There are arbitrary established systems and orders that govern man's well-being. In fact, a recent conclusion on the part of some notable scientists was cited on the front page of the *Wall Street Journal*, December 25, 2014: "Today there are more than 200 known parameters necessary for a planet to support life—every single one of which must be perfectly met, or the whole thing falls apart. … Due to these, we shouldn't be here. Yet here we are, not only existing, but talking about existing. What can account for it? The odds against life in the universe are simply astonishing. Can every one of those many parameters have been perfect by accident? At what point is it fair for science to admit that science suggests that we cannot be the result of random forces? Doesn't assuming that an intelligence created these perfect conditions require far less faith than believing that a life-sustaining Earth just happened to beat the inconceivable odds to come into being?"[1]

The advancements in science and technology make us more cognizant of the complexity of the universe, the world around us, and our human frame. The intricate irreducible systems within our bodies (e.g. the eye), which could not function should one of its lesser parts be absent, like the

---

1 Eric Metaxas, "Science Increasingly Makes the Case for God," *Wall Street Journal*, Posted: Dec. 25, 2014, at https://1ref.us/1uk, accessed 12/9/21.

parts of a mouse trap, point to the undeniable truth that they are the result of intelligent design. Each was designed for a specific role contributing to the overall synchronized marvelous machinery called the human body. The same is true in nature. There are ecosystems, which are a complex network, or biological community of coexisting and interacting living organisms. Each has a specific purpose and role essential to the interplay and operation of the other systems. One cannot exist or function without the other. They are all completely different from one another yet equal in value since they do not stand alone. Yet, their very uniqueness contributes to the overall functionality of the whole.

For centuries, mankind has dabbled with nature. Complete species of birds[2] and animals,[3] as well as parts of the ecosystem, have been decimated by those who assumed they were of no use, but only to discover that now there is an irreplaceable missing essential link in nature's chain.

Humanity, as a species, is also in jeopardy. Should the inherent natures of male and female be amalgamated, the existence of mankind would be in serious question—not by the dialectic of determinism to destroy one another but by the impact of the neutering of the sexes. By nature, a man is masculine, and a woman is feminine. Biologically and physiologically speaking, there are distinct differences between the two. These differences govern the well-being of society by the distinctiveness of a man and a woman as revealed in Holy Writ.

The tragedy occurs when an attempt is made to make the Bible say what it does not—just to make it seem supportive of a personal idea or notion. One example is in the matter of creation. A well-known theologian made the attempt to amalgamate Adam and Eve into one, stating, "So God created man in His own image, in the image of God created he him; male and female created he *him*" (Gen. 1:27). The inference is that man is both male and female. The first problem with this assertion is that the Bible does not say, "created He him," but, rather, "created He *them*." In other words, God made "Adam," which in Hebrew means a man, and then from Adam, He made an *ishah*, the Hebrew word for a woman. The text in question demonstrates the complete opposite of what the theologian asserted. God made *two* in His image: a distinct man, and from him, a distinct woman. Though the word "Adam," translated as "man," can at times be translated into the word "mankind," the sense of

---

2 Wikipedia, "List of recently extinct birds," at https://1ref.us/1ul, accessed 12/9/2021.
3 Endangered Species International, "Total number of extinct species: 905 (was 784 in 2006)," https://1ref.us/1um, accessed 12/9/2021.

the word is masculine. Therefore, since Eve was made from Adam, as it says: "Adam said, This *is* now bone of my bones, and flesh of my flesh: she shall be called Woman, because she was taken out of Man" (Gen. 2:23). The woman, by virtue of her origin, falls under the heading of man—that is, mankind. This contrasts with the idea that mankind comes from animals or from angels. The fact that God includes Eve as part of mankind does not blend the two into one, inasmuch as Adam existed as a man prior to the creation of the woman. The only time they are pronounced as being "one" is when God declared, "Therefore shall a man leave his father and his mother, and shall cleave unto his wife: and they shall be one flesh" (verse 24). Had they been created precisely at the same instant and had the union occurred immediately at her creation, this statement would have been unnecessary.

To be classified as a woman she must have all the components of a woman. She must have an ovum to be fertilized as well as the reproductive organs to facilitate insemination. She must also have the essential organs for the development of the fetus, providing all the necessary elements for the growth and complete maturation of a baby. A woman is born to develop breasts capable of producing milk for her offspring. This is not the rule with men.

> *Should the inherent natures of male and female be amalgamated, the existence of mankind would be in serious question—not by the dialectic of determinism to destroy one another but by the impact of the neutering of the sexes.*

Typically speaking, women and men are different in their emotions and in their thinking processes. Female hormonal patterns are more complex and varied. They have three physiological functions absent in males—menstruation, pregnancy, and lactation. Each of these influences her behavior and feelings significantly. Women are also more responsive emotionally. They laugh and cry more readily. A man will never be able to experience the precise feelings of a mother, and, conversely, a woman will never have the precise emotions and feelings of a father.

Following is a partial list of some of the notable differences between a man and a woman:

1. Because of her unique chromosomal pattern, a woman has greater constitutional vitality. Normally, women outlive men by three to four years. Generally, women die of disorders related to female reproduction and to breast cancer.
2. A woman's stomach, kidneys, liver, and appendix are larger than a man's. Their lungs are smaller than a man's, resulting in about thirty percent less lung capacity.
3. The basal metabolism of men is higher than that of women.
4. The first finger of a woman's hand is usually longer than the third; with men the reverse is usually true.
5. Boys' teeth last longer than do those of girls.
6. Women's skeletal structure has a shorter head, broader face, less protruding chin, shorter legs, and longer trunk.
7. The glands work differently in the two sexes. For example, a woman's thyroid is larger and more active; it enlarges during menstruation and pregnancy, which makes her more prone to goiter, provides resistance to cold, and is associated with the smooth skin, relatively hairless body, and the thin layer of subcutaneous fat that are important elements in the concept of personal beauty.
8. Her blood contains more water (20 percent fewer red cells). Since red cells supply oxygen to the body, she tires more easily and is more prone to fainting.
9. Normally, men are 50 percent stronger than women in brute strength.
10. Men's hearts beat slower than those of women (72 versus 80 beats per minute).
11. Women's blood pressure (ten points lower than men) varies more from minute to minute.
12. Women have menopause.
13. Women can withstand high temperatures better than men because their metabolism slows down less.
14. Men and women differ in every cell of their bodies because they carry a differing chromosomal pattern.[4]

---

4 Dr. James Dobson, "The Physical Differences Between Women and Men," https://1ref.us/1un, accessed 12/9/21.

15. Male and female fetus corpus callosum are different. The bridge of nerve tissue that connects the right and left sides of the brain has a thicker measurement in female fetuses than in male fetuses.[5]
16. In one experiment, men and women listened to a novel. "When males listened, only the left hemisphere of their brains was activated. The brains of female subjects, however, showed activity in both the left and right hemispheres."[6]
17. "Men have larger brains; women have more brain cells.
18. "Men and women use different parts of their brains while thinking.
19. "There are significant differences in the brain activity of men and women.
20. "Male brain neurons are about a third larger than female neurons; male and female neurons take up significantly different amounts of dopamine—a brain chemical that acts as a mood enhancer, relieves pain and regulates motion. …
21. "The electrical system of the heart is different in men and women: women have faster heart rates and a different electrocardiogram than a man."[7]

When it comes to the Creation, God could have done things differently. Instead of creating a man first, He could have very well done what He did with Mary the mother of Jesus (see Luke 1:29–35). He could have made Eve first and then planted in her a male seed. Nine months later, she would have given birth to Adam. This would have resulted in Eve being the first created human. Adam would then have been her son and subject to her rather than being her husband and she being subject to him.

But the story of Creation has a different twist, and the twist makes the story of Creation uniquely different from current notions about the sexes. God chose to create a man first (Gen. 2:7; 1 Tim. 2:13). After man's creation, God put him into a deep sleep and performed the first recorded surgery by opening up his side. He pulled out a bone and closed up the opening. (You can read the story in Gen. 2:21–23.) God then made a woman from the bone extracted from Adam. She is subsequently recorded after Adam and the description of her creation as the "mother

---

5 Lisa Collier Cool, "Are Male and Female Brains Different?" at https://1ref.us/1uo, accessed 12/9/2021.
6 Jomol, "Women are definitely from Earth, but where the Hell are men from," July 4, 2010, at https://1ref.us/1up, from www.medicinenet.com.
7 Dr. Marianne Legato, M.D., Ph.D., "Just The Facts," at https://1ref.us/1uq, accessed 12/9/2021.

of all living;" in turn, God called him Adam. Adam then called the woman "Eve" (Gen. 3:20).

This divine design suggests that God intended a certain order in the creation of mankind. If companionship were the primary factor in the creation of Eve, God could have created a Steve who would have been "closer than a brother" (Prov. 18:24) to Adam. But another male, though questionably satisfying the companionship issue that a woman can provide, would not have enabled Adam to fulfill God's command to "be fruitful and multiply" (Gen. 1:28), nor would two males have met the criteria provided in the Creation story that only a male and female can become one flesh in its true sense.

Another possible option was for God to make Eve precisely at the same time from the dust in the same exact way that He made Adam. Or, He could have made another male with female organs. But the fact that God made man first, then from the man He made the woman, explicitly and implicitly confirms and affirms that the woman was made for man, and not man for the woman, as Paul wrote, "Neither was the man created for the woman; but the woman for the man" (1 Cor. 11:9). It was a woman that God intended to meet the created natural intrinsic and inborn needs of a man and vice versa. Nothing else. They were made to have a symbiotic relationship with each other. How long during that day it took for Adam to sense his need of a companion after naming the animals in Genesis 2:19, 20, we don't know. But obviously, it took part of the day for Adam to realize, that unlike the other creatures, he was the only being of his kind.

Yet, what is recorded in Holy Writ is the fact that God first made Adam who initially had the sole responsibility to dress the garden (Gen. 2:15) and was admonished to avoid taking the fruit from the tree of the knowledge of good and evil (verses 16, 17) and called upon to name the animals (verses 19, 20). Adam was predominantly placed in his domain and given the stewardship or dominion of the entire earthly creation of God before the existence of the woman (Gen. 1:28; Ps. 8:4–8). Eve was subsequently added to Adam. Thus, at this stage, they were co-heirs of God's creation, with Adam as the leader of the pair.

Eve was created to be a "help meet" (Gen. 2:18, 20). This phrase is repeated twice for good reason. She was to help *him;* she was to be *his* assistant. And it was Adam who called her "Woman" (Gen. 2:23). From this point in the relationship, she was to be intimately tied to her husband and he to her (verse 24). While it is true that God made her from a bone close to his heart, equality was simply by reason of love, not by virtue of creation. In her standing as a woman, she was created just as perfect a woman as Adam was made a perfect man. Paul wrote the Galatians: "For as many of you as have been baptized into Christ have put on Christ. There is neither Jew nor Greek, there is neither bond nor free, there is neither male nor female: for ye are all one in Christ Jesus. And if ye *be* Christ's, then are ye Abraham's seed, and heirs according to the promise" (Gal. 3:27–29). When it comes to salvation, while remaining a Greek or a Jew, a man or a woman, a slave or freeman, all have equal access to Christ and His salvation. "For there is no difference between the Jew and the Greek: for the same Lord over all is rich unto all that call upon him" (Rom. 10:12). Nevertheless, God's admonition concerning the relationship that should exist in marriage of one toward the other is: "Likewise, ye husbands, dwell with *them* according to knowledge, giving honour unto the wife, as unto the weaker vessel, and as being heirs together of the grace of life; that your prayers be not hindered" (1 Peter 3:7). Spiritually speaking, they have mutual and equal heirship of "the grace of life;" they are equally sons and daughters of God.

Since Eve was not created as another man, then the comparison for the purpose of equality is senseless and becomes a moot issue. It would be like saying that an apple is equal to an orange, but the attempt to claim them equal is illogical. Thus, we have a distinct perfect man and a distinct perfect woman. Each with different bodies and abilities to perform different functions, with Adam being placed as the head. "For the husband is the head of the wife, even as Christ is the head of the church: and he is the saviour of the body" (Eph. 5:23). After the Fall, God said to the woman: "Thy desire *shall be* to thy husband, and he shall rule over thee" (Gen. 3:16).

Therefore, for the sake and well-being of the human race, God's ordained order must be maintained. These differences provide all of the known and yet unknown ingredients necessary for the birth, nurturing, stability, happiness, and existence of mankind.

2.

Uniquely Responsible and Responsibly Unique

W hen Eve fell to the delusions of Satan (Gen. 3:1–5), it was not yet considered that mankind had fallen. "And Adam was not deceived, but the woman being deceived was in the transgression" (1 Tim. 2:14). It was not until Adam yielded to Eve that the fall of man was accomplished. "For since by man *came* death, by man *came* also the resurrection of the dead. For as in Adam all die, even so in Christ shall all be made alive" (1 Cor. 15:21, 22; see also Job 31:33; Rom. 5:12–15). Adam (the one to whom God had given the dominion) was held responsible and charged with the fall, not Eve. "And the LORD God called unto Adam and said unto him, Where *art* thou" (Gen. 3:9). While both were hiding, God singled out the man, not the woman. "And he [Adam] said, I heard thy voice in the garden, and I was afraid, because I *was* naked; and I hid myself. And he said, Who told thee that thou wast naked? Hast thou eaten of the tree, whereof I commanded thee that thou shouldest not eat? ... And unto Adam He said, Because thou hast hearkened unto the voice of thy wife, and hast eaten of the tree, of which I commanded thee, saying, Thou shalt not eat of it: cursed *is* the ground for thy sake; in sorrow shalt thou eat *of* it all the days of thy life; thorns also and thistles shall it bring forth to thee; and thou shalt eat the herb of the field. In the sweat of thy face shalt thou eat bread, till thou return unto the ground; for out of it wast thou taken: for dust thou *art*, and unto dust shalt thou return" (Gen. 3:10, 11, 17–19).

The principal reason for this judgment upon Adam is specified in verses 11, 12, and 17, which read, "And he said, Who told thee that thou *wast* naked? Hast thou eaten of the tree, whereof I commanded thee that thou shouldest not eat? And the man said, The woman whom thou gavest *to be* with me, she gave me of the tree, and I did eat. ... And unto Adam he said, Because thou hast hearkened unto the voice of thy wife, and hast eaten of the tree, of which I commanded thee, saying, Thou shalt not eat of it." Adam obeyed the woman rather than God! Although God had put in place a chain of command—God to Adam and Adam to the woman, Adam circumvented that by putting the woman between him and God. By placing the woman above himself, he committed a flagrant violation of that which the Lord had ordered. It was—and still is—crucial to man's salvation and standing with God to absolutely obey His directives and maintain His order. To the men of ancient Israel, He said, "Now therefore, if ye will obey my voice indeed, and keep my covenant, then ye shall be a peculiar treasure unto me above all people: for all the earth is mine: And ye shall be unto me a kingdom of priests, and an holy nation. These are the words which thou shalt speak unto the children of Israel. And Moses came and called for the elders of the people, and laid before their faces all these words which the LORD commanded him" (Exod. 19:5–7). "But this thing commanded I them, saying, Obey my voice, and I will be your God, and ye shall be my people: and walk ye in all the ways that I have commanded you, that it may be well unto you" (Jer. 7:23). The act or practice of placing another ahead of God was the chief violation of Eve and Adam, and of the men of Israel that eventually brought down their nation and standing as a people with God.

> ❝ *Adam (the one to whom God had given the dominion) was held responsible and charged with the fall, not Eve.* ❞

Adam's fall brought about a chain-reaction of circumstances. "And the LORD God said, Behold, the man is become as one of us, to know good and evil: and now, lest he put forth his hand, and take also of the tree of life, and eat, and live for ever: Therefore the LORD God sent him forth from the garden of Eden, to till the ground from whence he was taken. So he drove out the man; and he placed at the east of the garden of Eden Cherubims, and a flaming sword which turned every way, to keep the way of the tree of life" (Gen. 3:22–24). Eve's banishment, while not mentioned, is inclusive in Adam's, due to her attachment to him. In His judgment, God zeroed in solely on Adam's violation, making no mention of the woman. Neither was she mentioned when God pronounced the potential of Adam becoming a lifelong sinner and the verdict of his eviction.

Concerning this, Paul wrote: "Wherefore, as by one man sin entered into the world, and death by sin; and so death passed upon all men, for that all have sinned: (For until the law sin was in the world: but sin is not imputed when there is no law. Nevertheless death reigned from Adam to Moses, even over them that had not sinned after the similitude of Adam's transgression, who is the figure of him that was to come. But not as the offence, so also *is* the free gift. For if through the offence of one many be dead, much more the grace of God, and the gift by grace, *which is* by one man, Jesus Christ, hath abounded unto many. ...)" (Rom. 5:12–15). To the Corinthians he wrote: "For as in Adam all die, even so in Christ shall all be made alive. But every man in his own order: Christ the firstfruits; afterward they that are Christ's at his coming" (1 Cor. 15:22, 23). Christ did not become a woman to rescue the human race. He became a man, and by becoming a man, He could rescue both the man and that which came from the man, the woman.

It is important to note that Eve's punishment was twofold: the hardship of childbearing, and the pronouncement that "thy desire *shall be* to thy husband, and he shall rule over thee" (Gen. 3:16). Adam's punishment was far more severe and extensive. The burden

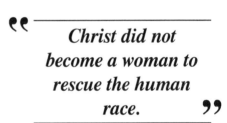

Christ did not become a woman to rescue the human race.

of the weight of the transgression placed on him was of a global nature. She was responsible for herself, while Adam was responsible for her and the world. While the promise of redemption was to involve both the man and the woman, it was she who was to give birth to the "seed" (Gen. 3:16), but it was the male seed that was to bring salvation to her and mankind. That Eve understood this was quite evident when, after the birth of Seth and in reference to the promised seed in Genesis 3:15, she said, "For God, *said she*, hath appointed me another seed instead of Abel, whom Cain slew" (Gen. 4:25). Though they had daughters born to them (see Gen. 5:4), the anticipated salvation had to come through the male child.

Consequently, the enemy of souls has misconstrued the purpose of the selection of the man-child for man's salvation. He has led many to consider the Bible as chauvinistic in nature because of the constant emphasis on the men. It is clear right from the start that the Scriptures begin with Adam and continue through the ten patriarchs leading to

Noah. The first genealogical list in Genesis chapter 4 solely traces the men from Cain's line. Chapter 5 exclusively mentions the male line of Seth, with brief inferences to "daughters" but with seldom a mention of wives. There is good reason for this lineup. Jews today trace their lineage by their mothers, this has gone on for "two thousand years of Jewish history."[8] However, prior to Christ, the genealogy was always traced by the fathers—it was by patrilineal descent. (See Genesis 4:16–22; 11:10–32; 1 Chron. 1:1–27; Luke 3:23–38.) Why was it by the father's line?

Eve's glee in having another son instead of Abel strongly attests to the fact that she understood her salvation to come through a man-child. "And Adam knew his wife again; and she bare a son, and called his name Seth: For God, *said she*, hath appointed me another seed instead of Abel, whom Cain slew. And to Seth, to him also there was born a son; and he called his name Enos: then began men to call upon the name of the LORD" (Gen. 4:25, 26). Consequently, since man's hope of salvation depended on an authentic and indisputable Messiah, it was imperative to track and earmark the Savior. That is why there are not only genealogies, but there are also over 300 prophecies to authenticate the Christ. He had to be of the male gender, born in a specific time and place, a direct descendant of Abraham, and traceable all the way back to God (see Luke 3:23–38).

Since the enemy of mankind has been desperately trying to ween men from the Savior, he will stop at nothing to allure men and women from Christ by deception, decoys, look-alikes, etc. Hence, Christ's warning about false Christs. "And then if any man shall say to you, Lo, here *is* Christ; or, lo, *he is* there; believe *him* not: For false Christs and false prophets shall rise, and shall shew signs and wonders, to seduce, if *it were* possible, even the elect" (Mark 13:21, 22).

"When the fulness of the time was come, God sent forth his Son, made of a woman, made under the law" (Gal. 4:4). Even after coming in direct fulfillment of Bible prophecy, Christ sought to convince His enemies of His genuineness by fulfilling the Bible prophecies. He said, "Thinkest thou that I cannot now pray to my Father, and he shall presently give me more than twelve legions of angels? But how then shall the scriptures be fulfilled, that thus it must be? In that same hour said Jesus to the multitudes,

8 Los Angeles Times Archives, "Rabbis Debate if Mothers Are Sole Path to Judaism : Lineage: Reform Jews confer religious identity through either parent. Orthodox and Conservative branches call that a 'tragic decision,' " Aug. 21, 1993, at https://1ref.us/1ur, accessed 12/9/2021.

Are ye come out as against a thief with swords and staves for to take me? I sat daily with you teaching in the temple, and ye laid no hold on me. But all this was done, that the scriptures of the prophets might be fulfilled. Then all the disciples forsook him, and fled" (Matt. 26:53–56). Among His own doubting followers, the same source of proof was also used. He said to them: "O fools, and slow of heart to believe all that the prophets have spoken: Ought not Christ to have suffered these things, and to enter into his glory? And beginning at Moses and all the prophets, he expounded unto them in all the scriptures the things concerning himself" (Luke 24:25–27). Inasmuch as the probability of one person fulfilling forty-eight Bible prophecies would be one chance in 10 to the 157th power[9] (that is, the number 10 with 157 zeros after it), His being the genuine Messiah by fulfilling 330 prophecies from the Old Testament is an even greater feat. This made it impossible for the devil or any mere human being to have accomplished it. Therefore, proof of His direct lineage to David and back to Adam was required in addition to fulfilling all the other prophecies. That is why Peter said, "Neither is there salvation in any other: for there is none other name under heaven given among men, whereby we must be saved" (Acts 4:12).

From this perspective, one can see God's wisdom in His sovereignty as the heavenly Father being for our salvation rather than a chauvinistic demeaning of womankind. Thus, mankind is to homogenously flourish as he maintains the order established by God in the Creation while continuing in this sinful environment inherited from Adam. Generally speaking, rules are not made to hinder good, but evil. Rules provide order and are the framework that gives form or substance to righteousness. They are hedges that provide containment and structure to keep the feet in the straight and narrow, leading to a life with the absence of the evils that frustrate man's happiness and bring his final demise. Within the established order ordained by God, man finds consistency, regularity, certainty, security, stability, peace, and eternal life. Outside of God's established rules and order, there is chaos, uncertainty, irregularity, instability, insecurity, lack of peace, and ultimately death.

Order is the primary reason why the Lord inspired Paul with the counsel: "Wives, submit yourselves unto your own husbands, as unto the Lord" (Eph. 5:22). He repeated the same to the Colossians: "Wives, submit yourselves unto your own husbands, as it is fit in the Lord. Husbands, love *your*

9 Peter Stoner, *Science Speaks,* Chicago: Moody Press, 1976, pp. 106–112, at https://1ref.us/1br, accessed 12/9/21.

wives, and be not bitter against them" (Col. 3:18). The word translated "submit" comes from the Greek word *hupotassō*, which is "a Greek military term meaning 'to arrange [troop divisions] in military fashion under the command of a leader.' "[10] In non-military use, it describes "a voluntary attitude of giving in, cooperating, assuming responsibility, and carrying a burden."[11] This word appears seven times in the writings of Paul, James, and Peter in the New Testament. Here are a couple of examples: "That ye submit yourselves unto such, and to every one that helpeth with us, and laboureth" (1 Cor. 16:16). "Obey them that have the rule over you, and submit yourselves: for they watch for your souls, as they that must give account, that they may do it with joy, and not with grief: for that *is* unprofitable for you" (Heb. 13:17).

Submission and not subordination is God's instruction to all true believers. "Submit yourselves therefore to God. Resist the devil, and he will flee from you." "Submit yourselves to every ordinance of man for the Lord's sake: whether it be to the king, as supreme." "Likewise, ye younger, submit yourselves unto the elder. Yea, all *of you* be subject one to another, and be clothed with humility: for God resisteth the proud, and giveth grace to the humble" (James 4:7; 1 Peter 2:13; 5:5). Paul's counsel was not intended to make a woman a slave or a servant, but rather for her to be a willing, trusting companion and an assistant to a man who is filled with the Spirit, Christlike, and capable of protecting, providing, and leading by love.

Abuses and wresting of the Scriptures have been a historical occurrence. Christ said to the Sadducees in His day, "Ye do err, not knowing the scriptures, nor the power of God" (Matt. 22:29). When the Pharisees and scribes asked, "Why walk not thy disciples according to the tradition of the elders, but eat bread with unwashen hands" (Mark 7:5), Jesus said: "Well hath Esaias prophesied of you hypocrites, as it is written, This people honoureth me with their lips, but their heart is far from me. Howbeit in vain do they worship me, teaching *for* doctrines the commandments of men. For laying aside the commandment of God, ye hold the tradition of men, *as* the washing of pots and cups: and many other such like things ye do. And he said unto them, Full well ye reject the commandment of God, that ye may keep your own tradition. For Moses said, Honour thy father and thy mother; and, Whoso curseth father or mother, let him die the death: But ye say, If a man shall say to his father

---

10 Kenneth Samuel Wuest, *First Peter in the Greek New Testament*, 1942, p. 60.
11 Marcus Barth, *Ephesians, The Anchor Bible*, 1974, p. 710.

or mother, *It is* Corban, that is to say, a gift, by whatsoever thou mightest be profited by me; *he shall be free*. And ye suffer him no more to do ought for his father or his mother; making the word of God of none effect through your tradition, which ye have delivered: and many such like things do ye" (Mark 7:6–13). If, in the very presence of the Creator, men dared to twist the Scriptures, it should be no surprise that the same distortion would continue even in this enlightened age. The apostle Peter wrote: "Even as our beloved brother Paul also according to the wisdom given unto him hath written unto you; as also in all *his* epistles, speaking in them of these things; in which are some things hard to be understood, which they that are unlearned and unstable wrest, as *they do* also the other scriptures, unto their own destruction" (2 Peter 3:15, 16). Paul warned: "For the time will come when they will not endure sound doctrine; but after their own lusts shall they heap to themselves teachers, having itching ears; And they shall turn away *their* ears from the truth, and shall be turned unto fables" (2 Tim. 4:3, 4).

God in mercy lays out before men and women examples of the positive or negative consequences when a man or a woman lives responsibly or irresponsibly and out of harmony with His will for them. In Proverbs, God paints a picture of a virtuous woman: "Who can find a virtuous woman? for her price *is* far above rubies" (Prov. 31:10; see also verses 11 through 29.)

Concerning His ideal of a man, He says: "Blessed *is* the man that walketh not in the counsel of the ungodly, nor standeth in the way of sinners, nor sitteth in the seat of the scornful. But his delight *is* in the law of the LORD; and in his law doth he meditate day and night. And he shall be like a tree planted by the rivers of water, that bringeth forth his fruit in his season; his leaf also shall not wither; and whatsoever he doeth shall prosper. The ungodly *are* not so: but *are* like the chaff which the wind driveth away. Therefore the ungodly shall not stand in the judgment, nor sinners in the congregation of the righteous. For the LORD knoweth the way of the righteous: but the way of the ungodly shall perish" (Ps. 1:1–6). And should any man have a question as to how this is possible, he need look no further than to the Perfect Pattern of Christ Jesus.

Sadly, both men and women are guilty of abrogating God's divine counsels and thus falling short of the glory of God. Men misuse the Bible to subjugate women into silent servitude or, by their own lack of spirituality, force women to step into a vacuum of the men's own making. On the other hand, some women, chafing under male dominance, seek to usurp the rightful position of men. Each have an inherent responsibility to maintain themselves within their God-ordained order, and, in so doing, fulfill God's purpose for each.

3.

Inspiration of The Bible as the Word of God

S ince the current issue is the suggestion that women be ordained to pastoral ministry by the church, the only logical place to find a solution is in the Bible. The spiritual nature of the church dictates that the rationale also be spiritual. Therefore, it is imperative to determine the level of inspiration to which the Scriptures can be trusted to clarify the matter.

Jesus used the Scriptures to correct wrongs in ideology and culture (see Matthew, chapters 4–7), to establish a truth, and to encourage faithfulness and obedience (see all the references below). He also pronounced the Word to be the only source of power over temptation (Matt. 4:1–10) and unequivocally declared it to be that which proceeded out of the mouth of God. Because Christ is the source of the Word and of life, Jesus confirms that "the words that I speak unto you, *they* are spirit, and *they* are life" (John 6:63). It is through the "exceeding great and precious promises" of the Word that we "might be partakers of the divine nature" and can escape "the corruption that is in the world through lust" (2 Peter 1:4). Moreover, it is by taking heed to the Word that "a young man can cleanse his way" (Ps. 119:9) and faith awakens by hearing the Word (Rom. 10:17). God never made it subject to twisting. On the contrary, it was to be the dissector. "For the word of God *is* quick, and powerful, and sharper than any two-edged sword, piercing even to the dividing asunder of soul and spirit, and of the joints and marrow, and *is* a discerner of the thoughts and intents of the heart" (Heb. 4:12).

Having such an element as this at our reach, I would certainly be afraid of any attempt to cut out any part of the Word as merely "culturally uninspired." The Scriptures are filled with many stories saturated with cultural issues, such as the contention between the wife and concubine of Abraham, and these are purposely not omitted by God from its pages. Since Christ declared all Scriptures to be the Word of God, it would be presumptuous for anyone to assume the impossible task of determining what parts are inspired and what parts are not. In spite of the warnings found in the Scriptures, people today still attempt to twist the Scriptures. It was true during the lifetime of the apostles as well. Peter wrote: "Our beloved brother Paul also according to the wisdom given unto him hath written unto you; as also in all *his* epistles, speaking in them of these things; in which are some things hard to be understood, which they that are unlearned and unstable wrest, as *they do* also the other scriptures, unto their own destruction" (2 Peter 3:15, 16).

Recently, a new hermeneutic has been introduced. (A hermeneutic is a method for determining the meaning of the biblical text.) It is called, "Principle-based-historical-cultural hermeneutics." It was introduced under the assumption that the Bible is " 'contaminated by the social, cultural, historical, and language' of the writer. So while the Scripture contains the truth, it needs an interpreter to distinguish between the divine principle and the prophet's 'baggage.' Therefore, Barna concludes that 'a plain reading of Scripture could be misleading.' "[12]

This new hermeneutic is disturbing. It presupposes that the ones using this mode of interpretation are sufficiently wise to determine what is inspired and what is not. It has been devised to clean away any apparently cultural statements *in contrast to feminist positions.* In other words, when Paul says, "Let your women keep silence in the churches" (1 Cor. 14:34), he is speaking out of his own cultural prejudice, which makes the statement uninspired. This position contradicts the explicit statement that declares all Scripture to be inspired.

Jesus warned the people of His day to be extremely careful how they handled His Word. Their salvation depended on their acceptance or rejection of His Word as our salvation does today. "Search the scriptures," He said, "for in them ye think ye have eternal life: and they are they which testify of me" (John 5:39). In the parable of the rich man and Lazarus, Jesus stated: "Abraham saith unto him, They have Moses and the prophets; let them hear them. ... And he said unto him, If they hear not Moses and the prophets, neither will they be persuaded, though one rose from the dead" (Luke 16:29, 31). From this perspective, how many verses of the Old Testament did Jesus caution His readers of having cultural biases, thereby corrupting the Scriptures? None! And the same Christ who inspired the Old Testament Scriptures, inspired all the New Testament.

---

12 Jan Barna, "Ordination of Women and the Two Ways to Unity: Ecclesiastical and Biblical," (presented to the *Adventist Society for Religious Studies*, Nov. 21, 2013), p. 4.

Those who assume that something cultural would make inspiration invalid should seriously reconsider that view. Throughout the writings of Moses, there are many things written about women, which, in those days, were cultural in nature. For example, the length of time of isolation given to a woman following the birth of a man child or a female child (Lev. 12:2–7). It would be well for a woman's health if this practice were still being followed today. There are many other practices or restrictions aimed solely at women in Leviticus that today would certainly be considered unacceptable (see Lev. 12; 15; 18; 19; 20; 21; Num. 5:11–31; 30:3–16; 31:17; Deut. 22:5; 22:13–21). These and other commands relating to women, as found in the Old Testament, though having cultural value, are now being stripped of their spiritual standing simply because they are now thought to undermine the ordination of women pastors. In the book of Job, inspiration records Job's friends' cultural biases. Though their conclusions were clearly contrary to God's counsel, they are nonetheless included by inspiration for future generations to learn from.

Paul, knowing the attacks that were coming upon Holy Writ, warned Timothy to "Preach the word; be instant in season, out of season; reprove, rebuke, exhort with all longsuffering and doctrine. For the time will come when they will not endure sound doctrine; but after their own lusts shall they heap to themselves teachers, having itching ears; And they shall turn away *their* ears from the truth, and shall be turned unto fables" (2 Timothy 4:2–4). He also explicitly wrote about the inspiration of the Scriptures. With apostolic authority he declared: "All scripture *is* given by inspiration of God, and *is* profitable for doctrine, for reproof, for correction, for instruction in righteousness: That the man of God may be perfect, thoroughly furnished unto all good works" (2 Timothy 3:16, 17).

The word "inspiration" in the Greek is *theopneustos*, which literally means, "God-breathed," or "God-inspired."[13] Peter contributed to the subject by explaining how "inspiration" was accomplished. He wrote, "Knowing this first, that no prophecy of the scripture is of any private interpretation. For the prophecy came not in old time by the will of man: but holy men of God spake *as they were* moved by the Holy Ghost" (2 Peter 1:20, 21).

In Paul's humble claims of inspiration, he unequivocally stated: "It is not expedient for me doubtless to glory. I will come to visions and revelations of the Lord. ... And lest I should be exalted above measure through

---

13 Francis D. Nichol, ed., *The Seventh-day Adventist Bible Commentary*, vol. 7, Washington, D.C.: Review and Herald Publishing Association, 1957, p. 344, commentary on 2 Timothy 3:16.

the abundance of the revelations, there was given to me a thorn in the flesh, the messenger of Satan to buffet me, lest I should be exalted above measure" (2 Cor. 12:1, 7). Paul frequently received direct personal communications from God (Acts 9:4–6; 16:9; 18:9, 10; 22:17, 18; 23:11; 27:23, 24; Gal. 2:2).

Knowing that Peter and Paul both believed the Bible to be God-inspired explains why they ardently defended and recommended God's Word and were willing to die for it. Paul's writings were based upon his understanding and dependence upon the Bible as the irrefutable Word of God. To the Romans he wrote: "Which He had promised afore by his prophets in the holy scriptures." "So then faith *cometh* by hearing, and hearing by the word of God." "For whatsoever things were written aforetime were written for our learning, that we through patience and comfort of the scriptures might have hope." "But now is made manifest, and by the scriptures of the prophets, according to the commandment of the everlasting God, made known to all nations for the obedience of faith" (Rom. 1:2; 10:17; 15:4; 16:26). It was to the Scriptures that he also pointed to convince the Jews that Christ was the *Sent* of God (Acts 13:16–41). "And Paul, as his manner was, went in unto them, and three sabbath days reasoned with them out of the scriptures. These were more noble than those in Thessalonica, in that they received the word with all readiness of mind, and searched the scriptures daily, whether those things were so" (Acts 17:2, 11). "And when they had appointed him a day, there came many to him into *his* lodging; to whom he expounded and testified the kingdom of God, persuading them concerning Jesus, both out of the law of Moses, and *out of* the prophets, from morning till evening" (Acts 28:23).

For the gentile Corinthian believers, it was essential that Paul provide anchoring in the only source of divine inspiration upon which they could turn to for clarity of faith and belief. He wrote, "For I delivered unto you first of all that which I also received, how that Christ died for our sins according to the scriptures; and that he was buried, and that he rose again the third day according to the scriptures" (1 Cor. 15:3, 4).

Inspiration is God's method of influencing and directing the minds of men in the process of making them channels of divine revelation. The word "inspiration" is found twice in the King James Version: in Job 32:8, where "inspiration" is *ruach*, which is literally "breath" in Hebrew, and in 2 Timothy 3:16, where the phrase, "All scripture is given by inspiration of God," in Greek, means that all scripture is "God-breathed." This is why Peter wrote: "The prophecy came not in old time by the will of man: but holy men of God spake *as they were* moved by the Holy Ghost" (2 Peter 1:20, 21; cf. Matt. 22:43; Mark 12:36; 1 Cor. 2:13; Heb. 3:7; etc.).

Many of the Old Testament scribes declared the inspiration of their message by prefacing or closing their statements with such words as "saith the Lord" (Isa. 1:24; Jer. 17:24; Amos 2:1; Zeph. 1:2, 3; Mal. 1:2; etc.), "the Lord spake thus" (Isa. 8:11), "the word of the Lord came unto me" (Ezek. 6:1; 7:1; 14:2; cf. Jonah 1:1; etc.), "the Lord said" (Hosea 1:2), and "the Lord hath spoken it" (Obadiah 1:18).[14]

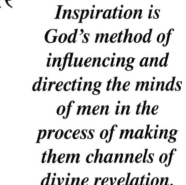

> *Inspiration is God's method of influencing and directing the minds of men in the process of making them channels of divine revelation.*

Because man's hope of salvation depended solely on the promised seed (Gen. 3:15; 13:15; Gal. 3:16), it was imperative that God should provide a way to guarantee the true seed. He did this through the inspired word, which is filled with prophecies, stories, illustrations, counsels, and types that only One could fulfill. That One was Christ. Christ attested to the inspiration of the Old Testament by referring to it as the word and record of God (Matt. 1:22, 23; 3:2, 3; 5:18; 21:42; Mark 1:2, 3; Luke 20:17, 18; John 2:15–17). Jesus also affirmed its authority by stating, "the scripture cannot be broken" (John 10:35). Paul claimed that what he taught was not "by human wisdom but ... by the Spirit" (1 Cor. 2:13, RSV; see 1 Cor. 7:40; 1 Thess. 2:13; 4:2, where he mentions his judgment), and Peter acknowledged Paul's writings as on par with "other scriptures" (2 Peter 3:16). The revelator claims that his message had its source in God and came to him through an angel (Rev. 1:1).[15]

Following are a few examples of Christ's attitude toward the inspiration of the Scriptures.

"Saying, The scribes and the Pharisees sit in Moses' seat" (Matt. 23:2).

14 Siegfried H. Horn, "Inspiration," *Seventh-day Adventist Bible Dictionary*, Washington, D.C.: Review and Herald Publishing Association, 1960, p. 504.
15 Siegfried H. Horn, "Inspiration," *Seventh-day Adventist Bible Dictionary*, Washington, D.C.: Review and Herald Publishing Association, 1960, p. 504.

"And saith unto him, See thou say nothing to any man: but go thy way, shew thyself to the priest, and offer for thy cleansing those things which Moses commanded, for a testimony unto them" (Mark 1:44).

"For Moses said, Honour thy father and thy mother; and, Whoso curseth father or mother, let him die the death" (Mark 7:10).

"And as touching the dead, that they rise: have ye not read in the book of Moses, how in the bush God spake unto him, saying, I *am* the God of Abraham, and the God of Isaac, and the God of Jacob?" (Mark 12:26).

"Abraham saith unto him, They have Moses and the prophets; let them hear them. And he said, Nay, father Abraham: but if one went unto them from the dead, they will repent. And he said unto him, If they hear not Moses and the prophets, neither will they be persuaded, though one rose from the dead" (Luke 16:29–31).

"Now that the dead are raised, even Moses shewed at the bush, when he calleth the Lord the God of Abraham, and the God of Isaac, and the God of Jacob" (Luke 20:37).

"And beginning at Moses and all the prophets, he expounded unto them in all the scriptures the things concerning himself. ... And he said unto them, These *are* the words which I spake unto you, while I was yet with you, that all things must be fulfilled, which were written in the law of Moses, and *in* the prophets, and *in* the psalms, concerning me" (Luke 24:27, 44).

"Jesus saith unto them, Did ye never read in the scriptures, The stone which the builders rejected, the same is become the head of the corner: this is the Lord's doing, and it is marvellous in our eyes?" (Matt. 21:42).

"Jesus answered and said unto them, Ye do err, not knowing the scriptures, nor the power of God" (Matt. 22:29).

"But how then shall the scriptures be fulfilled, that thus it must be? In that same hour said Jesus to the multitudes, Are ye come out as against a thief with swords and staves for to take me? I sat daily with you teaching in the temple, and ye laid no hold on me. But all this was done, that the scriptures of the prophets might be fulfilled. Then all the disciples forsook him, and fled" (Matt. 26:54–56).

"And Jesus answering said unto them, Do ye not therefore err, because ye know not the scriptures, neither the power of God?" (Mark 12:24).

"I was daily with you in the temple teaching, and ye took me not: but the scriptures must be fulfilled" (Mark 14:49).

"And beginning at Moses and all the prophets, He expounded unto them in all the scriptures the things concerning himself. And they drew nigh unto the village, whither they went: and he made as though he would have gone further. But they constrained him, saying, Abide with us: for it is toward evening, and the day is far spent. And He went in to tarry with them. And it came to pass, as he sat at meat with them, he took bread, and blessed *it*, and brake, and gave to them. And their eyes were opened, and they knew him; and he vanished out of their sight. And they said one to another, Did not our heart burn within us, while he talked with us by the way, and while he opened to us the scriptures? ... Then opened he their understanding, that they might understand the scriptures" (Luke 24:27–32, 45).

"Search the scriptures; for in them ye think ye have eternal life: and they are they which testify of me" (John 5:39).

"For had ye believed Moses, ye would have believed me: for he wrote of me" (John 5:46).

"Did not Moses give you the law, and *yet* none of you keepeth the law? Why go ye about to kill me? The people answered and said, Thou hast a devil: who goeth about to kill thee? Jesus answered and said unto them, I have done one work, and ye all marvel. Moses therefore gave unto you circumcision; (not because it is of Moses, but of the fathers;) and ye on the sabbath day circumcise a man. If a man on the sabbath day receive circumcision, that the law of Moses should not be broken; are ye angry at me, because I have made a man every whit whole on the sabbath day?" (John 7:19–23).

"And a certain Jew named Apollos, born at Alexandria, an elo-quent man, *and* mighty in the scriptures, came to Ephesus. ... For he mightily convinced the Jews, *and that* publickly, shewing by the scriptures that Jesus was Christ" (Acts 18:24, 28).

It is obvious that the writers of the Scriptures considered themselves inspired by God. It is also crystal clear that Jesus never even intimated that the Bible had any portion of it that was not inspired. Being the source himself, how could He cast even an inkling of a shadow of doubt upon its origin? His adamant stance regarding the unchangeable, unalterable, ever trustworthy inspiration of the Word He summed up in the statement: "Think not that I am come to destroy the law, or the prophets: I am not come to destroy, but to fulfil. For verily I say unto you, Till heaven and earth pass, one jot or one tittle shall in no wise pass from the law, till all be fulfilled" (Matt. 5:17, 18). The one "jot" in Greek is an *iota,* the ninth and smallest letter in the Greek alphabet, corresponding to the Hebrew *yod*, the smallest letter in the Hebrew alphabet, which is about the size of an English apostrophe. The *yod* is the first letter of the tetragrammaton— YHWH (the four Hebrew letters that stand in for the name of God). In essence, if you remove the *yod*, you remove God out of His Word. Christ is hereby declaring the immutability of His Word!

When seeking to understand the meaning of events or circumstances in life, prophets either quoted the Scriptures or searched and studied them. Daniel examined the writings of Jeremiah as divinely inspired (see Dan. 9:1, 2). The salvation of those who searched for biblical truth was critically dependent upon the absolute credibility of "every *word* that proceedeth out of the mouth of the LORD" (Deut. 8:3). "Of which salvation the prophets have inquired and searched diligently, who prophesied of the grace *that should come* unto you: Searching what, or what manner of time the Spirit of Christ which was in them did signify, when it testified beforehand the sufferings of Christ, and the glory that should follow" (1 Peter 1:10, 11).

It is through the Bible that mankind learns divine truth and is led to the God of their salvation. As it is written: "For whosoever shall call upon the name of the Lord shall be saved. How then shall they call on him in whom they have not believed? and how shall they believe in him of whom they have not heard? and how shall they hear without a preacher? And how shall they preach, except they be sent? as it is written, How beautiful are the feet of them that preach the gospel of peace, and bring glad tidings of good things! But they have not all obeyed the gospel. For Esaias saith, Lord, who hath believed our report? So then faith *cometh* by hearing, and hearing by the word of God" (Rom. 10:13–17). Therefore, it would stand to reason that the enemy of souls would attempt in some way to destroy confidence in the Bible or would suggest sufficient doubt, twist the Bible's meaning, or lead people to disregard it completely. The desire to use the Bible to support non-biblical alternative views is in itself unbiblical.

Following are statements that reveal the various ways that the enemy attempts to destroy the Scripture's influence. This is a compilation of several statements relative to the question of the inspiration of the Bible.

"There are some that may think they are fully capable with their finite judgment to take the Word of God, and to state what are the words of inspiration and what are not the words of inspiration. I want to warn you off that ground, my brethren in the ministry. 'Put off thy shoes from off thy feet, for the place whereon thou standest is holy ground.' There is no finite man that lives, I care not who he is or whatever is his position, that God has authorized to pick and choose in His Word.

"What man is there that dares to take that Bible and say this part is inspired and that part is not inspired? I would have both my arms taken off at my shoulders before I would ever make the statement or set my judgment upon the Word of God as to what is inspired and what is not inspired."[16]

"Those who think to make the supposed difficulties of Scripture plain, in measuring by their finite rule that which is inspired and that which is not inspired, had better cover their faces, as Elijah when the still small voice spoke to him; for they are in the presence of God and holy angels, who for ages have communicated to men light and knowledge, telling them what to do and what not to do, unfolding before them scenes of thrilling interest, waymark by waymark in symbols and signs and illustrations.

"And He [God] has not, while presenting the perils clustering about the last days, qualified any finite man to unravel hidden mysteries or inspired one man or any class of men to pronounce judgment as to that which is inspired or is not. When men, in their finite judgment, find it necessary to go into an examination of scriptures to define that which is inspired and that which is not, they have stepped before Jesus to show Him a better way than He has led us.

"I take the Bible just as it is, as the Inspired Word. I believe its utterances in an entire Bible. Men arise who think they find something to criticize in God's Word. They lay it bare before others as evidence of superior

---

16 E. G. White, Ms. 13, 1888, in *Sermons and Talks*, vol. 1, p. 65.

wisdom. These men are, many of them, smart men, learned men, they have eloquence and talent, the whole lifework [of whom] is to unsettle minds in regard to the inspiration of the Scriptures. They influence many to see as they do. And the same work is passed on from one to another, just as Satan designed it should be, until we may see the full meaning of the words of Christ, 'When the Son of man cometh, shall he find faith on the earth?' (Luke 18:8). Brethren, let not a mind or hand be engaged in criticizing the Bible. It is a work that Satan delights to have any of you do, but it is not a work the Lord has pointed out for you to do."[17]

"In almost every case where persons become unsettled in regard to the inspiration of the word of God, it is on account of their unsanctified lives, which that word condemns. They will not receive its reproofs and threatenings because these reflect upon their wrong course of action. They do not love those who would convert and restrain them. Difficulties and doubts which perplex the vicious heart will be cleared away before the one practicing the pure principles of truth."[18]

"The Holy Scriptures are to be accepted as an authoritative, infallible revelation of His will. They are the standard of character, the revealer of doctrines, and the test of experience. Spiritual darkness has covered the earth and gross darkness the people.... Many, very many, are questioning the verity and truth of the Scriptures. Human reasoning and the imaginings of the human heart are undermining the inspiration of the Word of God, and that which should be received as granted, is surrounded with a cloud of mysticism. Nothing stands out in clear and distinct lines, upon rock bottom. This is one of the marked signs of the last days....

"This Holy Book has withstood the assaults of Satan, who has united with evil men to make everything of divine character shrouded in clouds and darkness. But the Lord has preserved this Holy Book by His own miraculous power in its present shape—a chart or guidebook to the human family to show them the way to heaven."[19]

"In giving the word, 'holy men of God spake as they were moved by the Holy Ghost.' The word was not given at the option of men, and the use to be made of it is not left to their option. Men may not dissect or pronounce upon, wrest or misinterpret, take from or cast aside, any portion of that word according to their own judgment. Although its compilation, preservation, and transmission have been committed to men, it is wholly

17 E. G. White, Ms. 16, 1888, *Selected Messages*, bk. 1, p. 17.
18 E. G. White, *Testimonies to the Church*, vol. 1, p. 440.
19 E. G. White, *The Faith I Live By*, p. 13.

divine in its origin and in the thoughts expressed. It may not be demerited and pronounced upon by finite minds, because of its transmission through human agents."[20]

"Those who are truly converted to Christ [must] keep on constant guard lest they shall accept error in place of truth. Those who think that it matters not what they believe in doctrine, so long as they believe in Jesus Christ, are on dangerous ground. There are some who think that they will be just as acceptable to God by obeying some other law than the law of God—by meeting some other conditions than those He has specified in the gospel—as if they obeyed His commandments and complied with His requirements. But they are under a fatal delusion, and unless they renounce this heresy and come into harmony with His requirements, they cannot become members of the royal family."[21]

To divest the Scriptures of their inspiration is to remove from them the life-giving power inherent in the Word through the Holy Spirit. To attack the Word of God by diluting, twisting, or removing any portion of it is to rob the Scriptures of their sanctifying power. "There is no Bible sanctification for those who cast a part of the truth behind them. There is light enough given in the word of God, so that none need err."[22] Paul's departing words to those who would never see his face again were: "And now, brethren, I commend you to God, and to the word of his grace, which is able to build you up, and to give you an inheritance among all them which are sanctified" (Acts 20:32).

The man accredited to be the wisest among men wrote: "Every word of God *is* pure: he *is* a shield unto them that put their trust in him. Add thou not unto his words, lest he reprove thee, and thou be found a liar" (Prov 30:5, 6). The Lord said, "He that hath my word, let him speak my word faithfully. What is the chaff to the wheat? saith the LORD. *Is* not my word like as a fire? saith the LORD; and like a hammer *that* breaketh the rock in pieces? Therefore, behold, I *am* against the prophets, saith the LORD, that steal my words every one from his neighbour" (Jer. 23:28–30).

---

20 E. G. White, *The Bible Echo*, Aug 26, 1895.
21 E. G. White, *Christ Triumphant*, p. 235.
22 E. G. White, *Maranatha*, p. 89.

4.

Men Wrote the Bible

While participating in the 2014 General Conference Fall Council, I was alarmed at an attempt to neuter the Bible gender. The Fundamental Beliefs Committee presented word changes to some of the doctrines. One of them was in reference to 2 Peter 1:21, which reads: "For the prophecy came not in old time by the will of man: but holy men of God spake *as they were* moved by the Holy Ghost." The suggested word-change was to read, "Holy persons wrote as they were moved by the Holy Spirit."

Rising to my feet, I went to the microphone to address the issue. First, I asked if the reason for this change had anything to do with avoiding sexist language. They answered in the affirmative. Once I heard the affirmation for the rationale, I objected to the word-change and to another reason given, which was to "avoid causing confusion on the part of other Christian denominations relative to our doctrines." My response was that men in particular wrote the Bible. I stated that the Greek word was *anthropos*. *Anthropos* is either used to mean "mankind" or men. In this word, all living human beings are clumped under the men. It is never used in reference to womankind. The all-inclusive Greek word for "woman" is *gunē* (Strong's #1135). Biblically speaking, since the first woman was taken and made from a man's bone, all her offspring fall under the same origin. I then referred to Matthew 19:5–12, which reads, "And [Christ] said, For this cause shall a man [*anthropos*] leave father and mother, and shall cleave to his wife: and they twain shall be one flesh? Wherefore they are no more twain, but one flesh. What therefore God hath joined together, let not man [*anthropos*] put asunder. They say unto him, Why did Moses then command to give a writing of divorcement, and to put her away? He saith unto them, Moses because of the hardness of your hearts suffered you to put away your wives: but from the beginning it was not so. And I say unto you, Whosoever shall put away his wife, except *it be* for fornication, and shall marry another, committeth adultery: and whoso marrieth her which is put away doth commit adultery. His disciples say unto him, If the case of the man [*anthropos*] be so with *his* wife [*gune*], it is not good to marry. But he said unto them, All *men* cannot receive this saying, save *they* to whom it is given. For there are some eunuchs, which were so born from *their* mother's womb: and there are some eunuchs, which were made eunuchs of men: and there be eunuchs, which have made themselves eunuchs for the kingdom of heaven's sake. He that is able to receive *it*, let him receive *it*." *Anthropos* is definitely referring to men. However, if it is translated as "person," then a woman could be married to another woman, but this is a practice that is strictly forbidden in the entire Bible. Therefore, it was *men* who wrote the Bible.

In response to my statement, one of the committee members (a well-known scholar) went to the microphone and stated: "It is an assumption to say that only men wrote the Bible." "For," he said, "there is good evidence that Esther wrote the book of Esther." Unfortunately, no opportunity was given me to refute him. Upon my return home, I started doing some research in sources on the Internet, in the Bible, and in the writings of Ellen G. White, as well as consulting other scholars. My hunch was correct. I could find no evidence for the scholar's assertion. Thinking that perhaps he had resources that were not available to me, I wrote him, asking for evidence for the assertion. I said: "When there was a determined effort by the Fundamental Beliefs committee members to circumvent, bypass, reconstruct, or omit the language clearly written to avoid offending females, or to help other denominations not be confused about our biblical positions, the objective by this approach, in my estimate does not justify the wresting of the Scriptures. Will the committee choose to omit or change the wording in Scriptures concerning Sodomites, fornicators, adulterers, liars, thieves, etc., to avoid offense?"

The scholar wrote back with the following: "Yes, it is debatable whether Esther wrote the biblical book or not. But my point was and still is that you do find in the Bible portions written by women. Deborah coauthored a song with Barak and in this case she was the prophet (Judges 5:1–31). I specifically mentioned the case of the mother of Lemuel recorded in Proverbs 31:1–9. I can also add 'The Magnificat,' written by Mary found in Luke 1:46–55. My point was that we do find in the Bible passages originally written by women. I understood to be saying that only men wrote what we find in the Bible and based on what I know about the Bible I considered your statement not to be factual but an assumption. If I offended you by trying to clarify the issue I do sincerely apologize."

In retrospect, the thought came to me that to state that this particular text is sexist in nature is to incriminate the One who inspired the Bible as being sexist. Frankly, his email raised another concern. The suggestion about Deborah and Lemuel's mother and Mary was troubling.

The written response from the person who suggested "there was good evidence that Esther wrote the book of Esther," was: "It was debatable that Esther wrote the book of Esther." Then he proceeded to suggest that Deborah wrote part of the Bible, and that Mary's Magnificat, made her a contributing writer, as well as Lemuel's mother. The sad thing is that he plainly contended that "there was good evidence that Esther wrote the book of Esther." The issue at hand was the gender of the scribes of the Bible; not whether or not there were inserted speeches or writings that the writer of the book cited. Just as in this writing, I am quoting him. The mention of his statements does not make him the writer of this book. I am the one writing. I am the one citing him and others in this book.

In my response I wrote: "I have reread over the passages quoted to support your position. To suggest that Deborah being quoted trans-lates into her being a contributing writer of the Scriptures is to say that Balaam's story and recorded prophecies in Numbers chapter 22 to 24 could be construed to making him a contributing writer as well. The don-key that spoke to the dissolute prophet should also be included. There was Huram the king of Tyre in 2 Chronicles 2:1–16. Having his letter being recorded, according to your exegesis, would also make him a scribe of the Scriptures. But obviously, this is not the case. Others that fall into this category are: the writing of Elijah (2 Chron. 21:12–15), those of Cyrus (2 Chron. 36:22, 23), and of 'Bishlam, Mithredath, Tabeel, and the rest of their companions, unto Artaxerxes king of Persia' (Ezra 4:7–16); the writing of Ahasuerus (Esther 1:22), of Haman (Esther 3:12–15), the king's scribes letter dictated by Mordecai (Esther 8:9–14), king Darius' letter (Dan. 6:9, 10), or Pilate who said, 'What I have written, I have written' (John 19:19–22), Herod (Mark 6:14, 15), and King Agrippa (Acts 26:28–32), etc."

The scribes that the Lord chose were men who documented what occurred. They recorded who said what and who wrote what. The record-ing of the sayings or writings of others does not make those they refer to the biblical scribes but rather subject matter of the penmen. Therefore, "the Magnificat, spoken by Mary found in Luke 1:46–55," which you cite, has nothing to do with her writing, but rather speaking; and the writer of the book, which was Luke, was the one inspired to record it. I also reread

Proverbs 31:1–9. The wording begins: "The words of king Lemuel, the prophecy that his mother taught him." "You're suggesting that his mother is the author is incorrect. This is not saying that his mother wrote this in the Bible, but rather that King Lemuel himself is quoting the instruction of his mother. The verse reads literally, 'The words of Lemuel, king, a prophecy, which his mother taught him.' [Prov. 31:1.]"

A scan of the Bible reveals that the first order to write was to Moses (Exod. 17:14). The rest of the writings in the first five books of the Bible only refer to Moses' writing, with Deuteronomy 31:19 containing the last order to write in the Pentateuch. After that, 2 Chronicles 26:22 records what Isaiah wrote. In all the eighty-two verses of the Bible that the word "write" is used, it is only men who are commanded to write the words of the Lord. The other writings in the Bible, other than those that mention Jehovah, are subject matter mentioned or recorded by male prophets.

In searching the writings of Ellen G. White to find out whether she indicated, implied, or in any way inferred that women were contributors to the lists of biblical scribes, here is what I discovered: I found nothing in her writings to substantiate such a claim. On the contrary, she unequivocally makes clear that only men were the scribes of the Bible. Following are quotations I have selected that underscore this fact. In each quotation, I have marked in **bold** the specific language relative to the point at hand.

"By the plan of redemption, however, a way has been opened whereby the inhabitants of the earth may still have connection with heaven. **God has communicated with men by His Spirit**, and divine light has been imparted to the world by revelations to His chosen servants. '**Holy men of God** spake as they were moved by the Holy Ghost.' 2 Peter 1:21."[23] "We are to acknowledge His grace as made known through **the holy men of old**."[24]

"Eden, the home of Adam and Eve in their purity and innocence, came from the hand of the Creator a garden of perfect beauty; but this favored pair transgressed God's command, and were driven from the lovely home that had been prepared for them. Their sin and its sad consequences were put on record for our profit, to serve as a warning to those who should live after them. In the providence of God, samples of character are given us in his word, illustrating vice and virtue, sin and righteousness. **Inspired men**

23 E. G. White, *The Great Controversy*, p. v.
24 E. G. White, *The Desire of Ages*, p. 347.

wrote these histories, that we, viewing the characters of **these good men** as a whole, might copy their virtues and avoid their failures."[25]

"**Written in different ages, by men who differed widely in rank and occupation**, and in mental and spiritual endowments, the books of the Bible present a wide contrast in style, as well as a diversity in the nature of the subjects unfolded. Different forms of expression are employed by different writers; often the same truth is more strikingly presented by one than by another."

"God has been pleased to communicate His truth to the world by human agencies, **and He Himself, by His Holy Spirit, qualified men and enabled them to do this work.** He guided the mind in the selection of what to speak and what to write. The treasure was entrusted to earthen vessels, yet it is, nonetheless, from Heaven. The testimony is conveyed through the imperfect expression of human language, yet it is the testimony of God; and the obedient, believing child of God beholds in it the glory of a divine power, full of grace and truth."[26]

"The Bible points to God as its author; yet it was written by human hands; and in the varied style of its different books it presents the characteristics of the several writers. The truths revealed are all 'given by inspiration of God' (2 Timothy 3:16); **yet they are expressed in the words of men**. The Infinite One by His Holy Spirit has shed light into the minds and hearts of His servants. He has given dreams and visions, symbols and figures; and those to whom the truth was thus revealed have themselves embodied the thought in human language."[27]

"**The Scriptures were given to men,** not in a continuous chain of unbroken utterances, but piece by piece through successive generations, as God in His providence saw a fitting opportunity to impress man at sundry times and divers places. **Men** wrote as they were moved upon by the Holy Ghost. There is 'first the bud, then the blossom, and next the fruit,' 'first the blade, then the ear, after that the full corn in the ear.' This is exactly what the Bible utterances are to us."[28] "The Bible is written by **inspired men**, but it is not God's mode of thought and expression. It is that of humanity. God, as a writer, is not represented. Men will often say such an expression is not like God. But God has not put Himself in words, in

25 E. G. White, *Youth's Instructor*, Aug. 6, 1884.
26 E. G. White, *The Great Controversy*, pp. vi, vii.
27 E. G. White, *The Great Controversy*, p. v.
28 E. G. White, *Selected Messages,* bk. 1, p. 19.

logic, in rhetoric, on trial in the Bible. The writers of the Bible were God's penmen, not His pen. Look at the different writers."[29]

> ❝ *The Infinite One by His Holy Spirit has shed light into the minds and hearts of His servants. He has given dreams and visions, symbols and figures; and those to whom the truth was thus revealed have themselves embodied the thought in human language.* ❞

" 'Search the scriptures.' This is the word which comes to us from Christ. If it had been essential for us to search the [church] Fathers, Christ would have told us so. But the Fathers do not all speak the same thing. Which of them shall we choose as a guide? There is no need for us to trust to uncertainty. We pass by the Fathers to learn of God out of His Word. This is life eternal, to know God. Oh, how thankful we should be that the Bible is the inspired word of God. **Holy men of old wrote this Word as they were moved by the Spirit.** God did not leave His Word to be preserved in the memories of men and handed down from generation to generation by oral transmission and traditional unfolding. Had He done this, the Word would gradually have been added to by men. We would have been asked to receive that which is not inspired. Let us thank God for His written word."[30]

"In giving the word, '**holy men of God** spake as they were moved by the Holy Ghost.' The word was not given at the option of men, and the use to be made of it is not left to their option. Men may not dissect or pronounce upon, wrest or misinterpret, take from or cast aside, any portion of that word according to their own judgment. **Although its compilation, preservation, and transmission have been committed to men, it is wholly divine in its origin and in the thoughts expressed.** It may not be demerited and pronounced upon by finite minds, because of its transmission through human agents."[31]

"**It is not the words of the Bible that are inspired, but the men that were inspired.** Inspiration acts not on the man's words or his expressions

---

29 E. G. White, *Selected Messages,* bk. 1, p. 21.
30 E. G. White, *The Upward Look,* p. 52.
31 E. G. White, *The Bible Echo,* Aug. 26, 1895.

but on the man himself, who, under the influence of the Holy Ghost, is imbued with thoughts. But the words receive the impress of the individual mind. The divine mind is diffused. The divine mind and will is combined with the human mind and will; thus the utterances of the man are the word of God."[32]

"Wherever the will of God is violated by nations or by individuals a day of retribution comes. Many set aside the wisdom of God and prefer the wisdom of man and adopt some human invention or device. David placed the Word of God beside him on his throne. He was then immovable. But forsaking its doctrines he sullied one of the fairest reputations. **Turning from inspired men** and those who spread the Word before them praying God to shed light upon it, many make lies their refuge."[33]

These are only a few of the many statements supporting the truth that "holy men," not women, spoke and wrote as they were moved by the Holy Ghost.

---

32 E. G. White, *Selected Messages*, bk. 1, p. 21
33 E. G. White, *Manuscript Releases*, vol. 21, p. 169.

5.

Ordination in the Bible

T he practice of ordination seems elusive in the Old Testament since the word is not found there. What is found—three times—is the word "ordain." (See 1 Chron. 9:22; 17:9; Isa. 26:12.). Likewise, it is interesting to note that the word "baptism" is not found in the Old Testament. Why not? It is because the word "baptism" is of Greek origin, and, as such, it would not be found in writings written in Hebrew. Therefore, because the specific word "baptism" is not in the Old Testament, many people assume that the practice is solely of a New Testament origin. Were that actually the case, there would have been a question about John's baptizing. However, none asked, "Why are you submerging people in the water?" Instead, they asked, "Who are you?" They all knew and were acquainted with the practice of ceremonial immersion. The response of Peter on the day of Pentecost to the hearer's enquiry, "Men and brethren, what shall we do?" (Acts 2:37), was, "Repent, and be baptized" (verse 38). Also, the man of Ethiopia requested baptism (Acts 8:27–39) without Philip's mention of the practice. This makes it concretely clear that the ceremony was known and practiced by the Jews. It is obvious that Jews were well acquainted with the significance of baptism.[34] And it should also be clear that such is the case because Jews still baptize. "Although the term 'baptism' is not used to describe the Jewish rituals, the purification rites in Halakha Jewish law and tradition, called *tvilah*, have some similarity to baptism, and the two have been linked. The *tvilah* is the act of immersion in natural sourced water, called a mikva. In the Jewish Bible and other Jewish texts, immersion in water for ritual purification was established for restoration to a condition of 'ritual purity' in specific circumstances."[35]

That the longevity and indispensable nature of this ordinance played a crucial role in man's relationship to God is enforced by what Jesus said to Nicodemus the Pharisee: "Verily, verily, I say unto thee, Except a man

---

34 Henry F. Brown, *Baptism through the Centuries,* Pacific Press Publishing Assoc., 1965.
35 "History of baptism," https://1ref.us/1us, accessed 12/9/2021, citing Eric Stoltz, "Baptism," *A Christian Glossary. The Abraham Project,* accessed 2/25/2009; "Baptism," *Jewish Encyclopedia.*

be born of water and *of* the Spirit, he cannot enter into the kingdom of God. That which is born of the flesh is flesh; and that which is born of the Spirit is spirit" (John 3:5, 6). Jewish leaders recognized baptism as the rite for inducting proselytes into Judaism. "When therefore the Lord knew how the Pharisees had heard that Jesus made and baptized more disciples than John, (though Jesus himself baptized not, but his disciples,) He left Judaea, and departed again into Galilee" (John 4:1–3).

Christ stressed the essential nature and obvious longevity of this ceremony by His own example (Matt. 3:15–17), and, while addressing the refusal of the ordinance by the Pharisees and lawyers, He stated: "And all the people that heard *him*, and the publicans, justified God, being baptized with the baptism of John. But the Pharisees and lawyers rejected the counsel of God against themselves, being not baptized of him" (Luke 7:29, 30). He also reinforced the imperative and endurance of the spiritual cleansing during the institution of the ordinance of humility (John 13:5–10, 12–14). And prior to His ascension, He stated: "He that believeth and is baptized shall be saved; but he that believeth not shall be damned" (Mark 16:16).

The simple problem is that, in the Old Testament, the word or words used for the practice of baptism are "wash, cleanse, or purify." (See Genesis 35:1–5; Exodus 29:4; 40:12; Isaiah 1:16.) David wrote: "Wash me thoroughly from mine iniquity, and cleanse me from my sin. Purge me with hyssop, and I shall be clean: wash me, and I shall be whiter than snow" (Ps. 51:2, 7). There is an abundance of evidence in extra-biblical literature that the Jews practiced baptism throughout the ages. The Jews call it Tvilah.[36] "Tvilah" is the act of immersion in natural sourced water, called a "Mikva."[37] "Although the term '**baptism**' is not used to describe the **Jewish** rituals, the purification rites in **Jewish** law and tradition, **called** *tvilah*, have some similarity to **baptism**, and the two have been linked."[38]

What about the practice of ordination? Like baptism, ordination was also a practice in the Old Testament. It was the means that God (Christ) used to set men apart for a holy office of ministry. The first mention of ordination of an individual in the Old Testament is that of the priest Melchizedek, though nothing much is said about him other than that he met Abraham, blessed him, and received tithes from him (Gen. 14:18–20).

---

36 "History of baptism," at https://1ref.us/1us, accessed 8/28/2018.
37 Henry F. Brown, *Baptism Through the Ages*, Pacific Press Publishing Association, 1965.
38 "History of baptism," at https://1ref.us/1us, accessed 7/14/2020, boldfacing added.

Prior to the Aaronic priesthood, there were priests. Melchizedek and Jethro, Moses' father-in-law, are cited by name (see Gen. 14:18, Exod. 2:16; 3:1). Joseph's father-in-law, Potipherah, Priest of On, is also mentioned by name (Gen. 41:45, 50; 46:20). It is not debatable that these men holding the office of a priest were considered to be people of status. Beside these, there were other priests in Egypt, though they are not mentioned by name (see Gen. 47:22, 26), and there were priests among the children of Israel. Prior to giving the Ten Commandments, God said to Moses, "And let the priests also, which come near to the LORD, sanctify themselves, lest the LORD break forth upon them. ... And the LORD said unto him, Away, get thee down, and thou shalt come up, thou, and Aaron with thee: but let not the priests and the people break through to come up unto the LORD, lest he break forth upon them" (Exod. 19:22, 24). These priests were among the people prior to the establishment of the Aaronic priesthood. However, in the Bible there is no record about how these men became priests. Nevertheless, the reference to them strongly suggests that they were highly regarded and enjoyed a respect from the people as spiritual overseers. Concerning this recognition, Paul wrote about Melchizedek: "But he whose descent is not counted from them received tithes of Abraham, and blessed him that had the promises. And without all contradiction the less is blessed of the better" (Heb. 7:6, 7).

The time quickly came when, out of the rabble of semitic slaves in Egypt, God would organize a nation. For this purpose, He declared: "And ye shall be unto me a kingdom of priests, and an holy nation. These *are* the words which thou shalt speak unto the children of Israel" (Exod. 19:6). Prior to their departure from Egypt, the Lord commanded the Israelites to "borrow of her neighbour, and of her that sojourneth in her house, jewels of silver, and jewels of gold, and raiment" (Exod. 3:22; see also Exod. 11:2). Then God said, "Let them make me a sanctuary that I might dwell among them" (Exod. 25:8). Until this point, the beautiful materials that were to be used in the tabernacle were only common material (see verses 1–8). However, they were to be transformed from mere cloth and metals as they took the shape of God's dwelling place in the midst of Israel.

To this end, God ordered Moses to bring together what the people gave for the building of the sanctuary. Yet, in order to be utilized solely for a holy purpose, they must be made holy. To do so necessitated a holy agent to construct a dwelling that was likewise to be holy. So, Christ (2 Cor. 10:1–4) set apart Moses as the spiritual leader of Israel (Exod. 33:11; Num. 12:6–9). Then, "Moses took the anointing oil, and anointed the tabernacle and all that *was* therein, and sanctified them. And he sprinkled thereof upon the altar seven times, and anointed the altar and all his vessels, both the laver and his foot, to sanctify them" (Lev. 8:10, 11). The construction of the tabernacle and its furniture was complete, and ready for use. Its intended purpose and who would use it were still unknown until God revealed His plan. He declared. "Let them make me a sanctuary; that I may dwell among them" (Exod. 25:8).

By a command of God (Exod. 40:13–15), Aaron and his sons were then selected as the chosen vessels to minister in the sanctuary. They are the first in Scripture to be inducted into the priesthood through "anointing," which today we call "ordination." In this particular reference, God reveals something significant. Aaron, his sons, and their posterity were to serve for centuries as heads of the tabernacle of the congregation, which was, at times, called the sanctuary of the Lord. By command of God, Moses "poured of the anointing oil upon Aaron's head, and anointed him, to sanctify him" (Lev. 8:12). Aaron sons were also to be set apart in the same manner. "These *are* the names of the sons of Aaron, the priests which were anointed, whom he consecrated to minister in the priest's office" (Num. 3:3). "All priests were anointed, but the high priest only was anointed on the head; hence, by way of pre-eminence, he is here called 'the priest that is anointed' (see Ex. 29:7–9; Lev. 8:12, 13)."[39] There is something intriguing about the word "anointed." There are three Hebrew words for the English word in the Strong's Hebrew and Chaldee Dictionary. One word is *mâschah* (Strong's #4886), pronounced *maw-shakh'* and translated sixty-eight times as "anointed." It has the primary definition of "to smear, anoint, spread liquid." A second word for "anointed" is *mishchâh* (Strong's #4888). It is pronounced *meesh-khaw'* and translated twenty-four times as "anointing." Its primary definition is "consecrated portion, anointing oil, ointment." A third Hebrew word for "anointed" is *mâshîyach* (Strong's #4899), pronounced *maw-shee'-akh*. It is translated as "anointed" thirty-seven times and as "Messiah" two times.

One can well understand why anyone that knew Hebrew like David would show extreme caution when dealing with the Anointed One. David declared, "And he said unto his men, The LORD forbid that I should do this thing unto my master, the LORD'S anointed, to stretch forth mine hand against him, seeing he *is* the anointed of the LORD" (1 Sam. 24:6).

---

39 *The Seventh-day Adventist Bible Commentary*, vol. 1, p. 729, commentary on Leviticus 4:3.

David used the word *mashiyach* twice, which strongly suggests that this was not a mere man, but one set apart for a holy purpose functioning as the Messiah.

The anointing, or ordination, of Aaron and his sons was a permanent setting of them apart with responsibilities, authority, and restrictions. They were warned: "And ye shall not go out from the door of the tabernacle of the congregation, lest ye die: for the anointing oil of the LORD *is* upon you. And they did according to the word of Moses" (Lev. 10:7). God was specific! Only those of the tribe of Levi were set

> **"** *Aaron and his sons . . . . are the first in Scripture to be inducted into the priesthood through "anointing," which today we call "ordination."* **"**

apart by Him to participate in the sanctuary and its services. "These *are* the names of the sons of Aaron, the priests which were anointed, whom he consecrated to minister in the priest's office" (Num. 3:3). Any intruder into the sanctuary would pay for their trespass with their life (verse 10). God himself assigned specific chores for the Levites. None was to cross over the assignments ordered by the Lord. (See Numbers chapter 3). Aaron and his sons alone were to receive the offerings of the people, solely because they were signally set apart by ordination. We read, "And the LORD spake unto Aaron, Behold, I also have given thee the charge of mine heave offerings of all the hallowed things of the children of Israel; unto thee have I given them by reason of the anointing, and to thy sons, by an ordinance for ever" (Num. 18:8). These privileges were solely due to their anointing. "This *is the portion* of the anointing of Aaron, and of the anointing of his sons, out of the offerings of the LORD made by fire, in the day *when* he presented them to minister unto the LORD in the priest's office; which the LORD commanded to be given them of the children of Israel, in the day that he anointed them, *by* a statute for ever throughout their generations" (Lev. 7:35, 36).

Of special note is the process followed by Moses in setting apart those who, for a major portion of their lifetime, would do service on behalf of the people. By God's signaling out by name the ones He had chosen, it left no room for just anyone in Israel to fill those positions. In Numbers 3:3 we read, "These *are* the names of the sons of Aaron, the priests which were anointed, whom he consecrated to minister in the priest's office."

The word "consecration" is "the solemn dedication to a special purpose or service. The word *consecration* literally means 'association with the sacred.' Persons, places, or things can be consecrated, and the term is used in various ways by different groups. The origin of the word comes from the Latin stem *consecrat*, which means dedicated, devoted, and sacred. A synonym for to consecrate is to sanctify, a distinct antonym is to desecrate."[40] The particular mode of selection is worthy of notice as well. Moses was commanded, "Bring the tribe of Levi near, and present them before Aaron the priest, that they may minister unto him. And they shall keep his charge, and the charge of the whole congregation before the tabernacle of the congregation, to do the service of the tabernacle … Take the Levites instead of all the firstborn among the children of Israel, and the cattle of the Levites instead of their cattle; and the Levites shall be mine: I *am* the LORD" (Num. 3:6, 7, 45).

After all the Levites were assigned their respective duties for the sanctuary (see Numbers chapter 4), the entire congregation was brought together to publicly witness the setting apart of those whom God himself had selected to serve Him. "And thou shalt bring the Levites before the tabernacle of the congregation: and thou shalt gather the whole assembly of the children of Israel together: And thou shalt bring the Levites before the LORD: and the children of Israel shall put their hands upon the Levites: And Aaron shall offer the Levites before the LORD *for* an offering of the children of Israel, that they may execute the service of the LORD" (Num. 8:9–11). "For the LORD thy God hath chosen him [Levi] out of all thy tribes, to stand to minister in the name of the LORD, him and his sons for ever" (Deut. 18:5).

The anointing of the high priest was considered a permanent divine endorsement terminating at death. "And the congregation shall deliver the slayer out of the hand of the revenger of blood, and the congregation shall restore him to the city of his refuge, whither he was fled: and he shall abide in it unto the death of the high priest, which was anointed with the holy oil" (Num. 35:25). Unlike the high priest, the service of a Levitical priest would be for a period of time from the priest's thirtieth to fiftieth year (Num. 4:3). Once God ordained the chosen persons to serve as priests, any attempt to usurp them was to be met with death. "Therefore thou and thy sons with thee shall keep your priest's office for every thing of the altar, and within the veil; and ye shall serve: I have given your priest's

---

40 "Consecration," https://1ref.us/1ut, accessed 9/25/2020, adapted from "consecrate," in www.merriam-webster.com.

office *unto you* as a service of gift: and the stranger that cometh nigh shall be put to death" (Num. 18:7).

Consequently, irrespective of a person's position, the sacred rites were to be performed by no one other than the priests. Following is an example of a king attempting to do the rites of a priest and the ill consequences. "But when he [King Uzziah] was strong, his heart was lifted up to his destruction: for he transgressed against the LORD his God, and went into the temple of the LORD to burn incense upon the altar of incense. And Azariah the priest went in after him, and with him fourscore priests of the LORD, *that were* valiant men: And they withstood Uzziah the king, and said unto him, *It appertaineth* not unto thee, Uzziah, to burn incense unto the LORD, but to the priests the sons of Aaron, that are consecrated to burn incense: go out of the sanctuary; for thou hast trespassed; neither *shall it be* for thine honour from the LORD God. Then Uzziah was wroth, and *had* a censer in his hand to burn incense: and while he was wroth with the priests, the leprosy even rose up in his forehead before the priests in the house of the LORD, from beside the incense altar. And Azariah the chief priest, and all the priests, looked upon him, and, behold, he *was* leprous in his forehead, and they thrust him out from thence; yea, himself hasted also to go out, because the LORD had smitten him" (2 Chron. 26:16–20).

Moses' long life of arduous labor and burdens for the people of God was coming to an end. The faithful servant was about to be laid to rest, leaving an urgent need for the yet unfinished task of taking the nation of Israel into the Promised Land. And, although the established arrangement for setting up of the priesthood required the son to replace the father, with the replacement of Israel's human leader, this selection was different. The head of the nation, who would be under direct orders from God himself as Moses was, would be appointed by God. This selection must be made in such a way that no one would be left in doubt as to whom God would appoint and what authority the leader would have over the Lord's people. The manner by which this transference of the leadership and succession of command would be done mandated a public display for all to witness. Therefore, Moses, who in the eyes of the people had "shoes that no one could fill," must be the instrument used to establish his successor with unquestionable authority before the people. The God-chosen manner was not the typical earthly show of kingly physical power, prowess scheming, gallantry display, or fanfare. Rather it was a simple act ordained of Heaven by the laying on of hands. It was so solemn that the witnesses would be impressed of its sacred origin and divine appointment.

> *The God-chosen manner . . . . was a simple act ordained of Heaven by the laying on of hands. It was so solemn that the witnesses would be impressed of its sacred origin and divine appointment.*

"And the LORD said unto Moses, Take thee Joshua the son of Nun, a man in whom *is* the spirit, and lay thine hand upon him; And set him before Eleazar the priest, and before all the congregation; and give him a charge in their sight. And thou shalt put *some* of thine honour upon him, that all the congregation of the children of Israel may be obedient. And he shall stand before Eleazar the priest, who shall ask *counsel* for him after the judgment of Urim before the LORD: at his word shall they go out, and at his word they shall come in, *both* he, and all the children of Israel with him, even all the congregation. And Moses did as the LORD commanded him: and he took Joshua, and set him before Eleazar the priest, and before all the congregation: And he laid his hands upon him, and gave him a charge, as the LORD commanded by the hand of Moses" (Num. 27:18–23). By the simple act of the laying of Moses' hands, unquestionable authority was transferred to Joshua. "And Joshua the son of Nun was full of the spirit of wisdom; for Moses had laid his hands upon him: and the children of Israel hearkened unto him, and did as the LORD commanded Moses" (Deut. 34:9). Unlike the priests and kings that were anointed with oil (for Saul, see 1 Sam. 10:1; for David, 1 Sam. 16:13; 2 Sam. 5:3; for Solomon, 1 Kings 1:39), the laying on of hands would set Joshua apart. "Through the laying on of hands by Moses, accompanied by a most impressive charge, Joshua was solemnly set apart as the leader of Israel. He was also admitted to a present share in the government. The words of the Lord concerning Joshua came through Moses to the congregation, 'He shall stand before Eleazar the priest, who shall ask counsel for him, after the judgment of Urim before the Lord. At his word shall they go out, and at his word they shall come in, both he, and all the children of Israel with him, even all the congregation.' [Numbers 27] Verses 21–23."[41]

---

41 E. G. White, *Patriarchs and Prophets*, p. 463.

He was now the "acknowledged leader of Israel. He had been known chiefly as a warrior, and his gifts and virtues were especially valuable at this stage in the history of his people. Courageous, resolute, and persevering, prompt, incorruptible, unmindful of selfish interests in his care for those committed to his charge, and, above all, inspired by a living faith in God—such was the character of the man divinely chosen to conduct the armies of Israel in their entrance upon the Promised Land."[42]

God himself indisputably had pronounced His will relative to the high esteem placed on those who had been anointed or ordained. "When they were *but* a few men in number; yea, very few, and strangers in it. When they went from one nation to another, from *one* kingdom to another people; He suffered no man to do them wrong: yea, he reproved kings for their sakes; *Saying*, Touch not mine anointed, and do my prophets no harm" (Ps. 105:12–15). It was not a small matter for those kings to array themselves against men whom God had set apart. They were to beware how they treated God's servants that had been appointed or set apart by their anointing.

The secular spirit that abounds in society today has crept into the ranks of believers, resulting in the denuding of that which is sacred and making it common. Nevertheless, biblically speaking, those with spiritual discernment recognized this setting apart for a holy purpose and respected and honored it. Saul, the first king of Israel, was set apart by anointing to be the ruler of God's people. "Then Samuel took a vial of oil, and poured *it* upon his head, and kissed him, and said, *Is it* not because the LORD hath anointed thee *to be* captain over his inheritance?" (1 Sam. 10:1). David, likewise, was set apart through this God-chosen ordinance to succeed Saul. "Then Samuel took the horn of oil, and anointed him in the midst of his brethren: and the spirit of the LORD came upon David from that day forward. So Samuel rose up, and went to Ramah" (1 Sam. 16:13). David understood the significance of the divine appointment bestowed upon him by his anointing. To his wife, the daughter of Saul, he said, "*It was* before the LORD, which chose me before thy father, and before all his house, to appoint me ruler over the people of the LORD, over Israel" (2 Sam. 6:21).

Though King Saul sought David's life, David said of Saul, "The LORD forbid that I should do this thing unto my master, the LORD'S anointed, to stretch forth mine hand against him, seeing he *is* the anointed of the

---

42 E. G. White, *Patriarchs and Prophets*, p. 481.

LORD" (1 Sam. 24:6). So strong was his conviction concerning God's choosing by anointing that, though he was given the opportunity to rid himself of his enemy, he declared: "For who can stretch forth his hand against the LORD'S anointed, and be guiltless? ... The LORD forbid that I should stretch forth mine hand against the LORD'S anointed" (1 Sam. 26:9, 11). And, even after Saul's death (see 2 Sam. 1:14, 16, 21), David's recognition of the anointed of the Lord stood as a sharp rebuke to those that held as common what God had ordained.

Throughout the Scriptures, this setting apart by anointing was significant. None took it lightly. Many assume though, that, in the New Testament, God removed the sanctity of the ministry by removing the priesthood, thereby making every believer a priest. But this assumption is without merit or biblical support, as consideration of a few examples will show. God first set Jesus apart for a holy purpose. In regard to His being set apart by God, Jesus said, "The Spirit of the Lord *is* upon me, because he hath anointed me to preach the gospel to the poor; he hath sent me to heal the brokenhearted, to preach deliverance to the captives, and recovering of sight to the blind, to set at liberty them that are bruised, To preach the acceptable year of the Lord" (Luke 4:18, 19). This anointing Luke certified, quoting Peter, who said: "How God anointed Jesus of Nazareth with the Holy Ghost and with power: who went about doing good, and healing all that were oppressed of the devil; for God was with him" (Acts 10:38). The Greek word used in these two verses is *chriō*, pronounced *khree'-o*. It is #5548 in Strong's Greek Dictionary of the New Testament, which signified in the strongest manner the "consecrating of Jesus to the Messianic office."

Christ also set apart those who were to be elected as the leaders of the church. "And he ordained twelve, that they should be with him, and that he might send them forth to preach, And to have power to heal sicknesses, and to cast out devils" (Mark 3:14, 15). "And when it was day, he called *unto him* his disciples: and of them he chose twelve, whom also he named apostles" (Luke 6:13). The title of "apostle" lifted the twelve above all other disciples. They were the ones solely called "apostles," until later, when Paul was also included. "Paul, [he wrote] called *to be* an apostle of Jesus Christ through the will of God" (1 Cor. 1:1). Consequently, it is abundantly clear that Jesus considered them especially elevated by the frequent exercise of authority given them. "And when the hour was come, he sat down, and the twelve apostles with him" (Luke 22:14). It was in this upper room, while alone with the twelve men, that Jesus reminded them of their being set apart by ordination. He said, "Ye have not chosen me, but I have chosen you, and ordained you, that ye should go and bring forth fruit, and *that* your fruit should remain: that whatsoever ye shall ask of the Father in my name, he may give it you. These things I command you, that ye love one another" (John 15:16, 17).

That the other rank and file believers recognized the apostles' prominent status is clear even after the Resurrection when "Mary Magdalene, and Joanna, and Mary *the mother* of James, and other *women that were* with them, which told these things unto the apostles" (Luke 24:10). It was due to their election by Christ that the apostles became prominent in the New Testament church. "After that he through the Holy Ghost had given commandments unto the apostles whom he had chosen: To whom also he shewed himself alive after his passion by many infallible proofs, being seen of them forty days, and speaking of the things pertaining to the kingdom of God: And, being assembled together with *them*, commanded them that they should not depart from Jerusalem, but wait for the promise of the Father, which, *saith he*, ye have heard of me" (Acts 1:2–4). After the fulfillment of the promise of the Holy Spirit, Paul was later inspired to list the different spiritual gifts and offices in the church by order of importance. He wrote: "But all these worketh that one and the selfsame Spirit, dividing to every man severally as he will. ... And God hath set some in the church, first apostles, secondarily prophets, thirdly teachers, after that miracles, then gifts of healings, helps, governments, diversities of tongues" (1 Cor. 12:11, 28). The same chain of command of spiritual leadership Paul highlights in writing to the Ephesians, along with the purpose of their being given. "And he gave some, apostles; and some, prophets; and some, evangelists; and some, pastors and teachers; for the perfecting of the saints, for the work of the ministry, for the edifying of the body of Christ: till we all come in the unity of the faith, and of the knowledge of the Son of God, unto a perfect man, unto the measure of the stature of the fulness of Christ" (Eph. 4:11–13). Obviously, all believers were not apostles, prophets, pastors, or teachers. On the contrary, believers were the recipients of the ministry of those who were gifted to fulfil these roles.

When writing to the believers of Philippi, Paul felt no need to establish his authority as he did with other churches (e.g., 1 Cor. 1:1, 2; 2 Cor. 1:1; Gal. 1:1; Eph 1:10). He wrote, "Paul and Timotheus, the servants of Jesus Christ, to all the saints in Christ Jesus which are at Philippi, with the bishops and deacons" (Phil. 1:1). While the phrase "priesthood of all believers" is used to substantiate the nullification of the New Testament's ecclesiastical order, it betrays the reality of Christ's recognition of the church leadership that He established and ordained.

Significant is the fact that, as there were twelve patriarchs (Gen. 35:22; 49:28) and seventy elders selected in the Old Testament (see Exod. 6:14, 25; 12:21; 24:1, 9), so, likewise, did Christ select the same number in the New Testament. "After these things the Lord appointed other seventy also, and sent them two and two before his face into every city and place, whither he himself would come. ... Carry neither purse, nor scrip, nor shoes: and salute no man by the way. And into whatsoever house ye enter, first say, Peace *be* to this house. And if the son of peace be there, your peace shall rest upon it: if not, it shall turn to you again. And in the same house remain, eating and drinking such things as they give: for the labourer is worthy of his hire. Go not from house to house. And into whatsoever city ye enter, and they receive you, eat such things as are set before you: And heal the sick that are therein, and say unto them, The kingdom of God is come nigh unto you. But into whatsoever city ye enter, and they receive you not, go your ways out into the streets of the same, and say, Even the very dust of your city, which cleaveth on us, we do wipe off against you: notwithstanding be ye sure of this, that the kingdom of God is come nigh unto you. But I say unto you, that it shall be more tolerable in that day for Sodom, than for that city. Woe unto thee, Chorazin! woe unto thee, Bethsaida! for if the mighty works had been done in Tyre and Sidon, which have been done in you, they had a great while ago repented, sitting in sackcloth and ashes. But it shall be more tolerable for Tyre and Sidon at the judgment, than for you. And thou, Capernaum, which art exalted to heaven, shalt be thrust down to hell. He that heareth you heareth me; and he that despiseth you despiseth me; and he that despiseth me despiseth him that

> *While the phrase "priesthood of all believers" is used to substantiate the nullification of the New Testament's ecclesiastical order, it betrays the reality of Christ's recognition of the church leadership that He established and ordained.*

sent me. And the seventy returned again with joy, saying, Lord, even the devils are subject unto us through thy name" (Luke 10:1, 4–17).

Ecclesiastical authority was primarily extended to the twelve. While ministering among them Jesus said, "Moreover if thy brother shall trespass against thee, go and tell him his fault between thee and him alone: if he shall hear thee, thou hast gained thy brother. But if he will not hear *thee, then* take with thee one or two more, that in the mouth of two or three witnesses every word may be established. And if he shall neglect to hear them, tell *it* unto the church: but if he neglect to hear the church, let him be unto thee as a heathen man and a publican. Verily I say unto you, Whatsoever ye shall bind on earth shall be bound in heaven: and whatsoever ye shall loose on earth shall be loosed in heaven" (Matt. 18:15–18). Then, prior to His ascension, He reaffirmed the authority vested in them. "Then said Jesus to them again, Peace *be* unto you: as *my* Father hath sent me, even so send I you. And when he had said this, he breathed on *them*, and saith unto them, Receive ye the Holy Ghost: Whose soever sins ye remit, they are remitted unto them; *and* whose soever *sins* ye retain, they are retained" (John 20:21–23). "And Jesus came and spake unto them, saying, All power is given unto me in heaven and in earth. Go ye therefore, and teach all nations, baptizing them in the name of the Father, and of the Son, and of the Holy Ghost: Teaching them to observe all things whatsoever I have commanded you: and, lo, I am with you alway, *even* unto the end of the world" (Matt. 28:18–20).

"The lapse of time has wrought no change in His parting promise to His apostles as He was taken up from them into heaven: 'Lo, I am with you alway, even unto the end of the world' (Matthew 28:20). He has ordained that there should be a succession of men who derive authority from the first teachers of the faith for the continual preaching of Christ and Him crucified. The Great Teacher has delegated power to His servants, who 'have this treasure in earthen vessels.' Christ will superintend the work of His ambassadors if they wait for His instruction and guidance."[43]

Paul's recognition of the authority vested in him enabled him to remind the believers of the sacred role he performed as a minister. He wrote: "Let a man so account of us, as of the ministers of Christ, and stewards of the mysteries of God" (1 Cor. 4:1). "We then, *as* workers together *with him*, beseech *you* also that ye receive not the grace of God in vain. (For he saith, I have heard thee in a time accepted,

---

43 Ellen G. White, *Lift Him Up*, p. 175.

and in the day of salvation have I succoured thee: behold, now *is* the accepted time; behold, now *is* the day of salvation.) Giving no offence in any thing, that the ministry be not blamed: But in all *things* approving ourselves as the ministers of God, in much patience, in afflictions, in necessities, in distresses" (2 Cor. 6:1–4). "From Miletus he [Paul] sent to Ephesus, and called the elders of the church. And when they were come to him, he said unto them, Ye know, from the first day that I came into Asia, after what manner I have been with you at all seasons, serving the Lord with all humility of mind, and with many tears, and temptations, which befell me by the lying in wait of the Jews: *and* how I kept back nothing that was profitable *unto you*, but have shewed you, and have taught you publickly, and from house to house, testifying both to the Jews, and also to the Greeks, repentance toward God, and faith toward our Lord Jesus Christ. And now, behold, I go bound in the spirit unto Jerusalem, not knowing the things that shall befall me there: Save that the Holy Ghost witnesseth in every city, saying that bonds and afflictions abide me. But none of these things move me, neither count I my life dear unto myself, so that I might finish my course with joy, and the ministry, which I have received of the Lord Jesus, to testify the gospel of the grace of God. And now, behold, I know that ye all, among whom I have gone preaching the kingdom of God, shall see my face no more. Wherefore I take you to record this day, that I *am* pure from the blood of all *men*. For I have not shunned to declare unto you all the counsel of God. Take heed therefore unto yourselves, and to all the flock, over the which the Holy Ghost hath made you overseers, to feed the church of God, which he hath purchased with his own blood" (Acts 20:17–28).

The apostles did the same to the handpicked elders. "And when they had ordained them elders in every church, and had prayed with fasting, they commended them to the Lord, on whom they believed" (Acts 14:23). The solemn charge given by the apostle Paul to Timothy, "Lay hands suddenly on no man" (1 Tim. 5:22), strongly suggests and implies the sacredness of this heavenly established manner of setting apart men for holy service in the church.

To Titus, Paul stressed the level of authority placed on men who were to serve the church as elders. He wrote: "Paul, a servant of God, and an apostle of Jesus Christ, according to the faith of God's elect, and the acknowledging of the truth which is after godliness; In hope of eternal life, which God, that cannot lie, promised before the world began; But hath in due times manifested his word through preaching, which is committed unto me according to the commandment of God our Saviour; To Titus, *mine* own son after the common faith: Grace, mercy, *and* peace, from God the Father and the Lord Jesus Christ our Saviour. For this cause left I thee in Crete, that thou shouldest set in order the things that are wanting, and ordain elders in every city, as I had appointed thee: If any be blameless, the husband of one wife, having faithful children not accused of riot or unruly. For a bishop must be blameless, as the steward of God; not selfwilled, not soon angry, not given to wine, no striker, not given to filthy lucre; But a lover of hospitality, a lover of good men, sober, just, holy, temperate; Holding fast the faithful word as he hath been taught, that he may be able by sound doctrine both to exhort and to convince the gainsayers" (Titus 1:1–9).

When writing to the Thessalonians, Paul unreservedly made clear the level of responsibility and authority he possessed. In admonishing tones, he wrote, "And that ye study to be quiet, and to do your own business, and to work with your own hands, as we commanded you" (1 Thess. 4:11). In his second letter to the Thessalonians, he restated his position as having authority to lead and command the believers. "For yourselves know how ye ought to follow us: for we behaved not ourselves disorderly among you; Neither did we eat any man's bread for nought; but wrought with labour and travail night and day, that we might not be chargeable to any of you: Not because we have not power, but to make ourselves an ensample unto you to follow us. For even when we were with you, this we commanded you, that if any would not work, neither should he eat. For we hear that there are some which walk among you disorderly, working not at all, but are busybodies. Now them that are such we command and exhort by our Lord Jesus Christ, that with quietness they work, and eat their own bread. But ye, brethren, be not weary in well doing. And if any man obey not our word by this epistle, note that man, and have no company with him, that he may be ashamed. Yet count *him* not as an enemy, but admonish *him* as a brother" (2 Thessalonians 3:7–15).

The conditions stipulated concerning one who would become a bishop, or elder, were very clear. "The office of elder was too sacred and important for a hasty admission or re-admission of anyone who had not proved himself worthy. The candidate for eldership must first be carefully examined as to his qualifications."[44] These conditions are set forth in 1 Timothy 3:1–7. "This *is* a true saying, If a man desire the office of a bishop, he desireth a good work. A bishop then must be blameless, the husband of one wife, vigilant, sober, of good behaviour, given to hospitality, apt to teach; not given to wine, no striker, not greedy of filthy lucre; but patient, not a brawler, not covetous; one that ruleth well his own house, having his children in subjection with all gravity; (For if a man know not how to rule his own house, how shall he take care of the church of God?) Not a novice, lest being lifted up with pride he fall into the condemnation of the devil. Moreover he must have a good report of them which are without; lest he fall into reproach and the snare of the devil."

The same is true for the deacon. "Likewise *must* the deacons *be* grave, not double-tongue, not given to much wine, not greedy of filthy lucre; Holding the mystery of the faith in a pure conscience. And let these also first be proved; then let them use the office of a deacon, being *found* blameless. Even so *must their* wives *be* grave, not slanderers, sober, faithful in all things. Let the deacons be the husbands of one wife, ruling their children and their own houses well. For they that have used the office of a deacon well purchase to themselves a good degree, and great boldness in the faith which is in Christ Jesus" (1 Tim. 3:8–13). In both cases, each was to be a man, not a woman. The word "wife," in Greek, is the word *gune*, which is the word used for women in general. This particular word clarifies, without epicenity ("the lack of gender distinction"), the intent of God relative to the gender of both an elder and a deacon.

It was by divine election that God specifically chose Aaron and his sons, who were males, and not Miriam, who was a female, to serve as priests (Exod. 40:13–15; 1 Chron. 23:13). This was in spite of the protest and sin of Miriam (Num. 12:1–9), Korah and his 250 self-proclaimed priests (Num. 16:1–35), and the multitude. The same was true of the twelve disciples in the New Testament. Christ "calleth *unto him* whom he would" (Mark 3:13). It is by divine election, an election that only He could have annulled. However, rather than doing so, He established it as a perpetual order for His church and its believers.[45]

---

44 *The Seventh-day Adventist Bible Commentary*, vol. 7, p. 314, commentary on 1 Timothy 5:22.
45 Watch "1. Reflections on the Ordination Controversy—Louis Torres—Women's Ordination Symposium," available at https://1ref.us/1uu, accessed 1/2/2022.

Marvelous and quite significant are the words written in the final book of the Bible. "And the wall of the city had twelve foundations, and in them the names of the twelve apostles of the Lamb" (Rev. 21:14). The apostles' high status and recognition by Christ is unceasing. Their God-given authority will continue throughout eternity, showing the assurance of God's declaration—"For I *am* the Lord, I change not" (Mal. 3:6)!

6.

Subaudition Language Since God did not say that it couldn't be done, then it must be ok!

A mother needed to go out to the local store.

"Johnny," she said, pointing at the front door, "I don't want you to go out that door. You understand?"

"Yes, Mom!" responded Johnny.

While mother was gone, Johnny got a chair to climb out of a window. Sister said, "Johnny, didn't mother tell you not to go out?"

"She said not to go out the door, but she never said that I could not go out the window!" he exclaimed.

> **Sister said, "Johnny, didn't mother tell you not to go out?"**

Did mother have to say, I don't want you to go out the window, the basement, the attic, or the garage, in order to make herself clear? Or was it sufficient to simply state what she wanted and by so doing eliminate any other option? I think you will agree that Johnny understood his mother's subaudition wishes, but, in order to do what he wanted, he sought to justify his actions by suggesting to his sister that his actions were based on what she did not say.

When it comes to the Bible, most people are not aware that God at times uses subaudition language. What is subaudition language? According to Webster's dictionary, "it is a thing not stated, only implied, or inferred." It is used by making an explicit command and leaving no room for any other alternative.

Perhaps you have heard someone say, "God did not say that we cannot smoke, therefore, as far as He is concerned, it must be okay to smoke." Or maybe you have heard it said, with reference to the subject at hand, "God does not say that women cannot be pastors. Therefore, women pastors must be permissible." This rationalization may appear to justify people's sidestepping what God apparently does say by what He does not say. And, if there were no subaudition mandates, the notion might be justifiable. But in light of what is revealed, God at times uses subaudition, or tacit (unstated but implied) language, and by doing so, makes no room for any exception, making the imperative even stronger than if clearly stated. Let me give some examples.

> " *"She said not to go out the door, but she never said that I could not go out the window!" he exclaimed.* "

Several of the rooms in my house needed painting. Because of time constraints and a necessary trip, there was no time for me to do it myself. To get the job done, I called and hired a man to do it. When he arrived, I let him know that the outside of an unpainted wall on the backside of the house needed to be painted in "Swedish coffee." The walls inside the laundry room I wanted in semi-gloss white, and the walls in the kitchen I wanted in semi-gloss white paint, and the trimmings in black. While I was away, he sent me pictures of the job done inside the laundry room and kitchen. What a change a fresh coat of paint can make! Now, tell me, in order to give directions to the man, did I need to tell him that I did not want the rooms painted in red, nor in blue, nor in yellow, nor in brown, nor in green? No! My clear instructions regarding my desire for the color of each wall automatically implied negation of anything other than what I stipulated.

What if I were to ask my son to help me dig a hole in the right-hand corner of the backyard so I could plant an apple tree, and then I were to take him to the back of the yard and show him the marked-out spot? What would I expect him to do? Need I specify what I do *not* want, or should it be sufficient to just express what I *do* want? Let's say, then, that he returns to me after a while and tells me the job is completed, and then I go get the tree out of my truck and head to the specified spot. But, behold, when I get to the spot, there is no hole there. So, I call my son and ask him, "Didn't you say you were done?"

"Yes," he says.

"Where is the hole?" I ask.

"It's in the right-hand corner of the front yard," he responds. "I made a nice deep hole, and it is ready for the tree."

Now, tell me, did I need to say, "Do not dig the hole in the front left-hand corner of the front yard, nor in the center of the front yard, nor in the right-hand corner of the front yard, nor in the left-hand corner of the back yard?" No, of course not! My specific directions omit any other option. If he did not follow my specific directions, he dug *his* hole, not mine.

Now, let's look at some biblical examples of this principle. God declared: "And on the seventh day God ended his work which he had made; and he rested on the seventh day from all his work which he had made. And God blessed the seventh day, and sanctified it: because that in it he had rested from all his work which God created and made" (Gen. 2:2, 3). Later on, the seventh day is set apart as holy in the Scriptures and included in a command, which God wrote in stone: "Remember the sabbath day, to keep it holy. Six days shalt thou labour, and do all thy work: But the seventh day *is* the sabbath of the LORD thy God: *in it* thou shalt not do any work, thou, nor thy son, nor thy daughter, thy manservant, nor thy maidservant, nor thy cattle, nor thy stranger that is within thy gates: For *in* six days the LORD made heaven and earth, the sea, and all that in them *is*, and rested the seventh day: wherefore the LORD blessed the sabbath day, and hallowed it" (Exod. 20:8–11). He declared the seventh-day Sabbath to be a "holy convocation" (Lev. 23:3) and made its observance a "perpetual covenant" (Exod. 31:16; Ezek. 46:3; Isa. 66:23). Did He need to have said: The Sabbath is not the first day (Sunday), nor the second day (Monday), nor the third day (Tuesday), etc.? No! By stating which day He meant, He subauditionally omitted any other possibility.

Something that is implied in Holy Writ can be either positive or negative. But, usually, implied or inferred prohibitions are made by a positive assertion. For example, "For *in* six days the LORD made heaven and earth, the sea, and all that in them *is*, and rested the seventh day" (Exod. 20:11; see also 31:17). This statement has two tacit elements. One is the omission of any other possible length of time for the planet's creation, and the other is, as already stated, that no other day besides the seventh day is the Sabbath. The Lord said, "Remember the Sabbath day to keep it holy" (Exod. 20:8). The implied prohibition is obvious. Only one day is holy; all other days are not (see Exod. 20:8–11; Gen. 2:1–4). God says, "My day is holy." Yet, some people say, "Every day is holy." Who is right?

Here is another illustration. God made one woman for the first man. This assignment implies that man is to practice monogamy—that is, that he should have only one wife. Yet, polygamy was and still is practiced. Why? Because some of the patriarchs set unfortunate examples by practicing polygamy, which, by departing from God's created order, have been the cause of centuries of rivalry and bloodshed. Yet, today, some of particular religious persuasions assert, "There is no place where God explicitly forbids it." Why then did Jesus state, in response to the inquiry about divorce: "Have ye not read, that he which made *them* at the beginning made them male and female, and said, For this cause shall a man leave father and mother, and shall cleave to his wife: and they twain shall be one flesh? [Notice it does not say "his wives!"] Wherefore they are no more twain, but one flesh. What therefore God hath joined together, let not man put asunder. They say unto him, Why did Moses then command to give a writing of divorcement, and to put her away? He saith unto them, Moses because of the hardness of your hearts suffered you to put away your wives: but from the beginning it was not so. And I say unto you, Whosoever shall put away his wife, except *it be* for fornication, and shall marry another, committeth adultery: and whoso marrieth her which is put away doth commit adultery" (Matt. 19:3–9). Jesus quoted Genesis 2:24, and, in so doing, removed any doubt as to what God intended from the beginning, and He revealed man's perfidy in sidestepping a clear mandate stated in a subauditional tone to get his way.

Let's look at another instance. God gave a directive to Noah: "Of every clean beast thou shalt take to thee by sevens, the male and his female: and of beasts that *are* not clean by two, the male and his female" (Gen. 7:2). The positive mandate left no room for selecting any other number of pairs of the clean other than seven. The same is true of the unclean—one pair of each. The implication negates any other selection than that designated. By God's declaration, making some animals clean and others unclean, He locked in their designation. That is why Noah followed the tacit instruction given. When he made a sacrificial offering for the great deliverance, he only did so with those designated as clean (Gen. 8:20). And while people in Noah's day made other choices and might have preferred something other than what God had offered, there was only one ark of safety.

Another illustration. "Thou shalt have a place also without the camp, whither thou shalt go forth abroad: And thou shalt have a paddle upon thy weapon; and it shall be, when thou wilt ease thyself abroad, thou shalt dig therewith, and shalt turn back and cover that which cometh from thee" (Deut. 23:12, 13). The relieving had to be followed precisely as ordered. They had to mark out a place *outside* the camp to relieve themselves. No one questions the importance of hygiene and sanitation here concerning what God meant, and conversely, what He did not mean.

Let's consider the time of the giving of the manna. Moses wrote: "This *is* the thing which the LORD hath commanded, Gather of it every man according to his eating, an omer for every man, *according to* the number of your persons; take ye every man for *them* which *are* in his tents. And the children of Israel did so, and gathered, some more, some less. And when they did mete *it* with an omer, he that gathered much had nothing over, and he that gathered little had no lack; they gathered every man according to his eating. And Moses said, Let no man leave of it till the morning" (Exod. 16:16–19). Some decided to circumvent God's directive. The record states: "Notwithstanding they hearkened not unto Moses; but some of them left of it until the morning, and it bred worms, and stank: and Moses was wroth with them" (verse 20).

Let's look at another example. Since God says that an elder is a man, can anything else be an elder? Here are some examples: God tells Moses to meet with the elders in Egypt, which were the fathers of Israel (Exod. 3:16, 17). Elders at Passover were male heads of their families (Exod. 12:21). The seventy elders under Moses were men, which were heads and "officers" over the people (Num. 11:16, 24; Judges 21:16). In the New Testament, the same gender of an elder continues in Israel (Acts 25:15). It also continues among God's faithful (bishop, or elder, 1 Tim. 3:1, 2). And Paul, after making it well-defined that an elder should only have one wife, admonishes the believers with these words: "Let the elders that rule well be counted worthy of double honour, especially they who labour in the word and doctrine. Against an elder receive not an accusation, but before two or three witnesses" (1 Tim. 5:17, 19).

Since God calls men elders in His Word, does that allow for something else to be called an elder? God calls a man, "father." It would be therefore unthinkable for the children to call him "mother" or, conversely, to call the woman "father." A switch in the titles would be diametrically opposite to the fifth commandment.

You may wonder, then, why does a church have women as elders if there is no biblical example nor support? The movement to make women pastors has failed in three General Conference Sessions. It did not receive support in the 1990 and 1995 sessions. Again, the attempt was renewed and reintroduced in the 2000 GC Session. Once again, it failed. Then the pro-women supporters came up with a different strategy. In 1985, unordained pastors in the United States had been granted permission to perform the sacraments (the Lord's Supper, baptism, weddings, and funerals) due to an Internal Revenue Service's ruling that refused to give parsonage exclusion to unordained pastors unless they were permitted to do the sacraments. The decision was made to permit unordained pastors to perform the ceremonies under the condition that they must be ordained as a local elder, and they must only perform those services in the church of their assignment and that only in North America.

This provided an open door to reach their goal by a circuitous route. At a Fall Council in 1984, the Annual Council reaffirmed the 1975 Spring Meeting action that women can be ordained as local church elders in those divisions which make provision for it.[46] The request was made under the plea that in certain churches either men were unwilling to do the work of an elder, or there were no men to serve as an elder. Not realizing where this would lead, the request was granted. It did not take long for women to be elected as elders, whether or not there were men to serve. And since an elder must be ordained to officiate over the sacraments, women began to be ordained. Once they were ordained, they began to do the sacraments. Once there were enough women performing the rites, the strong position they had hoped for would have been gained. Women were then placed in pastoral positions performing the rites in their own local churches. This then created a strong momentum for the movement. Consequently, since there had been a variance already established in the North American Division to permit unordained pastors to perform the sacraments, which gave women elders the right to also perform the rites, the request was once again solicited to grant another variance where each division of the General Conference could determine their own policy on this matter. The issue was introduced and debated at the General Conference in 2015. Once again, the church voted down the suggestion.

In His Word, God gives several examples of those who have been given explicit orders and the sad outcome of taking another route. The Lord said to Balaam, "Thou shalt not go with them; thou shalt not curse the people: for they *are* blessed" (Num. 22:12). But Balaam's coveting the honor and promised wealth led him to seek a circulative way to go. In refusing his request three times, the Lord did not subauditionally mean that he could possibly, perhaps, maybe, perchance, feasibly, or imaginably go and curse them. The final end of Balaam is recorded in Joshua 13:22 as a warning and admonition to those who choose a different course besides that which the Lord intends in His directives. So strong is the Lord's hatred of this clever and surreptitious tendency that Balaam is made an

---

46 "Has General Conference Session approved ordained female church elders?" Nov. 17, 2017, at https://1ref.us/1uv, accessed 8/16/21.

example in the book of Revelation as a dangerous chameleon subversive to the faith. Jesus said: "I have a few things against thee, because thou hast there them that hold the doctrine of Balaam, who taught Balac to cast a stumblingblock before the children of Israel, to eat things sacrificed unto idols, and to commit fornication" (Rev. 2:14).

Another example is in the story of the first king of Israel, which is a tragic tale. God gave King Saul several directives with implications through the prophet Samuel. Though he fully understood what was implied, he chose to carry out his own will rather than do what the Lord specifically directed him to do. A perfect example is given in 1 Samuel 15:17–23. Because of his failure to follow God's instructions, the prophet Samuel uttered the stinging words to King Saul: "Behold, to obey *is* better than sacrifice, and to hearken than the fat of rams. For rebellion *is as* the sin of witchcraft, and stubbornness *is as* iniquity and idolatry. Because thou hast rejected the word of the LORD, he hath also rejected thee from *being* king" (1 Sam. 15:22, 23). Isaiah likewise declared: "Woe unto *them that are* wise in their own eyes, and prudent in their own sight" (Isa. 5:21)! The wisest of men wrote: "The way of a fool *is* right in his own eyes: but he that hearkeneth unto counsel *is* wise" Prov 12:15).

The situation today is not unlike the days of the prophet Jeremiah. During that time, the people would do anything besides what God had specifically counseled. "And they have built the high places of Tophet, which *is* in the valley of the son of Hinnom, to burn their sons and their daughters in the fire; which I commanded *them* not, neither came it into my heart" (Jer. 7:31). Well did the prophets warn those back then, as well as those of today, who have been unwilling to accept God's election in their adding to what God did not say!

This principle carries through in the New Testament. Prior to his death, Jesus made the promise: "Let not your heart be troubled: ye believe in God, believe also in me. In my Father's house are many mansions: if *it were* not *so*, I would have told you. I go to prepare a place for you. And if I go and prepare a place for you, I will come again, and receive you unto myself; that where I am, *there* ye may be also" (John 14:1–3). By this statement, Jesus comforted His disciples with the clear proposition that, at the Second Advent and not immediately at death, they would be united with their Lord. (See John 6:39, 40, 44, 53–58; 1 Thess. 4:13–17.)

If God says, "Do this!" it implies that there is no other alternative unless He provides the alternative. When a certain lawyer asked Jesus, "Master, what shall I do to inherit eternal life? He said unto him, What is written in the law? how readest thou? And he answering said, Thou shalt love the Lord thy God with all thy heart, and with all thy soul, and with all thy strength, and with all thy mind; and thy neighbour as thyself. And he said unto him, Thou hast answered right: this do, and thou shalt live" (Luke 10:25–28). There is no ambiguity here. Though not explicitly stated, the man knew what Christ implied. "But he, willing to justify himself, said unto Jesus, And who is my neighbour" (verse 29).

As Jesus' death was nearing, the system of sacrifices was meeting its antitype. Christ was about to go to the cross and, by His death, do away with the ceremonial system that symbolized His atonement for the sins of the world. In this crucial hour of transition from the Old Covenant to the New, He must make it absolutely clear what parts of the old system of types and shadows would be done away with or replaced (see Dan. 9:27; Col. 2:14–17; Heb. 8:6–13; 9:1–13). It is important to take special note that there is no record of Christ stating that He was replacing the sacrificing of animals with the emblems of His body. By simply implementing this new ceremony called the Lord's Supper or communion, the great majority of the Christian world has accepted the implied change of the system of sacrifices.

No one but the originator Himself had the authority to change what had been instituted. Therefore, whatever was going to be altered must be done prior to His death. "For where a testament *is*, there must also of necessity be the death of the testator. For a testament *is* of force after men are dead: otherwise it is of no strength at all while the testator liveth" (Heb. 9:16, 17). There must be no ambiguity. Therefore, choosing the absolute method to implement the change, He utilized the positive assertion, making clear what was intended and implied and leaving no room for any other option. "And he took bread, and gave thanks, and brake *it*, and gave unto them, saying, This is my body which is given for you: this do in remembrance of me. Likewise also the cup after supper, saying, This cup *is* the new testament in my blood, which is shed for you" (Luke 22:19, 20).

The emblems chosen for the continuance of the Lord's supper are recorded. The Lord said, "And he took the cup, and gave thanks, and said, Take this, and divide *it* among yourselves: For I say unto you, I will not drink of the fruit of the vine, until the kingdom of God shall come. And he took bread, and gave thanks, and brake it, and gave unto them, saying, This is my body which is given for you: this do in remembrance of me. Likewise also the cup after supper, saying, This cup *is* the new testament in my blood, which is shed for you" (Luke 22:17–20). The bread was unleavened bread. "The fourteenth day of the second month at even they shall keep it, *and* eat it with unleavened bread and bitter *herbs*" (Num. 9:11). These emblems, unleavened bread without the bitter herbs, replaced the killing and eating of the lamb, together with the "fruit of the vine," which is new wine, or what we today call grape juice. It would be sacrilege to use any other food or drink than what the Lord subauditionally ordained.

In legal matters, all legal contracts have to have terms that are clear. Therefore, such contracts use the phrase, "expressed or implied," to cover what is meant and what is not meant.

The apostle Paul confirmed the implementation of this ceremony in 1 Corinthians 11:23–26. He wrote: "For I have received of the Lord that which also I delivered unto you, That the Lord Jesus the *same* night in which he was betrayed took bread: And when he had given thanks, he brake *it*, and said, Take, eat: this is my body, which is broken for you: this do in remembrance of me. After the same manner also *he took* the cup, when he had supped, saying, This cup is the new testament in my blood: this do ye, as oft as ye drink *it*, in remembrance of me. For as often as ye eat this bread, and drink this cup, ye do shew the Lord's death till he come." The institution of the Lord's Supper replaced the Passover, not by a list of what *not* to do, but simply by a command of what *to* do, making obvious the restrictions implied.

Through the apostle Peter, the Lord confirms the role of a minister as being male-directed and, by inference, as omitting women. "As every man hath received the gift, *even so* minister the same one to another, as good stewards of the manifold grace of God. If any man speak, *let him speak* as the oracles of God; if any man minister, *let him do it* as of the ability which God giveth: that God in all things may be glorified through Jesus Christ, to whom be praise and dominion for ever and ever. Amen" (1 Peter 4:10, 11).

There are those who argue that the Bible does not specifically say that a woman cannot be a pastor, therefore, there is nothing wrong with it. This assertion would be correct if God had not already specified what He *did* want. "When choosing seventy elders to share with him the responsibilities of leadership, Moses was careful to select, as his helpers, men possessing dignity, sound judgment, and experience. In his charge to these elders at the time of their ordination, he outlined some of the qualifications that fit a man to be a wise ruler in the church. 'Hear *the causes* between your brethren,' said Moses, 'and judge righteously between *every* man and his brother, and the stranger *that is* with him. Ye shall not respect persons in judgment; *but* ye shall hear the small as well as the great; ye shall not be afraid of the face of man; for the judgment *is* God's.' Deuteronomy 1:16, 17."[47]

The same principles of piety and justice that were to guide the rulers among God's people, in the time of Moses and of David, were also to be followed by those given the oversight of the newly organized church of God in the gospel dispensation. In the work of setting things in order in all the churches and ordaining suitable men to act as officers, the apostles held to the high standards of leadership outlined in the Old Testament Scriptures. They maintained that those who are called to stand in a position of leading responsibility in the church must be noble pious men. Paul wrote: "For this cause left I thee in Crete, that thou shouldest set in order the things that are wanting, and ordain elders in every city, as I had appointed thee: If any be blameless, the husband of one wife, having faithful children not accused of riot or unruly. For a bishop must be blameless, as the steward of God; not selfwilled, not soon angry, not given to wine, no striker, not given to filthy lucre; But a lover of hospitality, a lover of good men, sober, just, holy, temperate; Holding fast the faithful word as he hath been taught, that he may be able by sound doctrine both to exhort and to convince the gainsayers" (Titus 1:5–9).

To make arrangements for the Old Testament tabernacle and its services, God said: "And take thou unto thee Aaron thy brother, and his sons with him, from among the children of Israel, that he may minister unto me in the priest's office, *even* Aaron, Nadab and Abihu, Eleazar and Ithamar, Aaron's sons. And thou shalt make holy garments for Aaron thy brother for glory and for beauty. And thou shalt speak unto all *that are* wise hearted, whom I have filled with the spirit of wisdom, that they may make Aaron's garments to consecrate him, that he may minister unto me in the priest's office" (Exod. 28:1–3). "And no man taketh this honour unto himself, but he that is called of God, as *was* Aaron" (Heb. 5:4). This is a holy calling—not a career, a form of employment, or a job. And the calling extends beyond the Old Testament and transcends the ages, for it states, "he that is called of God, as *was* Aaron." The text also suggests a masculine selection as was Aaron, and Christ—hence the usage of "no man" takes the honor "unto himself" (Greek *eautō*, which is masculine).

It is important also to note that there were other priests before Aaron. God said, "And let the priests also, which come near to the LORD,

47 Ellen G. White, *The Acts of the Apostles*, p. 94.

sanctify themselves, lest the LORD break forth upon them. And Moses said unto the LORD, The people cannot come up to mount Sinai: for thou chargedst us, saying, Set bounds about the mount, and sanctify it. And the LORD said unto him, Away, get thee down, and thou shalt come up, thou, and Aaron with thee: but let not the priests and the people break through to come up unto the LORD, lest he break forth upon them" (Exod. 19:22–24).

For those who sought to follow in the counsels of God, painstaking efforts were taken to abide by what had been ordained relative to the role of Aaron and his lineage. Korah's great rebellion in encouraging others to take up the priesthood and the 250 princes' daring act of offering incense—an act that should only have been carried out by the designated priests—brought God's indignation, which struck fear in the hearts of the people. "And the LORD spake unto Moses, saying, Speak unto Eleazar the son of Aaron the priest, that he take up the censers out of the burning, and scatter thou the fire yonder; for they are hallowed. The censers of these sinners against their own souls, let them make them broad plates *for* a covering of the altar: for they offered them before the LORD, therefore they are hallowed: and they shall be a sign unto the children of Israel. And Eleazar the priest took the brazen censers, wherewith they that were burnt had offered; and they were made broad *plates for* a covering of the altar: *To be* a memorial unto the children of Israel, that no stranger, which *is* not of the seed of Aaron, come near to offer incense before the LORD; that he be not as Korah, and as his company: as the LORD said to him by the hand of Moses" (Num. 16:36–40). Add to this the tragic death of Uzza a few centuries later (see 1 Chron. 13:9, 10), which was a painful reminder of the failure to carry out God's intent. These sharp rebukes caused king David to handle the things of God precisely as God had ordered. Aaron and his sons alone had the singular responsibility of handling the ark. "Their brethren also the Levites were appointed unto all manner of service of the tabernacle of the house of God. But Aaron and his sons offered upon the altar of the burnt offering, and on the altar of incense, and were appointed for all the work of the place most holy, and to make an atonement for Israel, according to all that Moses the servant of God had commanded" (1 Chron. 6:48, 49).

Those who were faithful descendants of David followed the same orders. "Then Hezekiah the king rose early, and gathered the rulers of the city, and went up to the house of the LORD. And they brought seven bullocks, and seven rams, and seven lambs, and seven he goats, for a sin offering for the kingdom, and for the sanctuary, and for Judah. And he commanded the priests the sons of Aaron to offer *them* on the altar of the LORD" (2 Chron. 29:20, 21).

This established order of the role of Aaron and his descendants was sacredly chronicled and guarded. Entire genealogies were maintained throughout the Old Testament dispensation (see 1 Chron. 6:3–57) to ensure that only males of Aaron's line could serve in the ministry. "These were reckoned by their genealogy in their villages, whom David and Samuel the seer did ordain in their set office" (1 Chron. 9:22). The same was true in the days of King Hezekiah, about 250 years later: "Beside their genealogy of males, from three years old and upward, *even* unto every one that entereth into the house of the LORD, his daily portion for their service in their charges according to their courses; Both to the genealogy of the priests by the house of their fathers, and the Levites from twenty years old and upward, in their charges by their courses; And to the gene- alogy of all their little ones, their wives, and their sons, and their daugh- ters, through all the congregation: for in their set office they sanctified themselves in holiness: Also of the sons of Aaron the priests, *which were* in the fields of the suburbs of their cities, in every several city, the men that were expressed by name, to give portions to all the males among the priests, and to all that were reckoned by genealogies among the Levites" (2 Chron. 31:16–19). All others were prohibited from serving.

After the destruction of Judah as an empire, while in the twenty-fifth year of the Jews' captivity, Ezekiel the prophet (c. 572 A.D) was given a vision of a future temple, and those who would officiate in its services. He wrote: "And thou shalt give to the priests the Levites that be of the seed of Zadok, which approach unto me, to minister unto me, saith the Lord GOD, a young bullock for a sin offering" (Ezek. 43:19). After the broad scattering of the Jewish people throughout the known world and the sub- sequent great migration back to Jerusalem, records were still being kept in this regard. "And these *were* they which went up from Telmelah, Telharsa, Cherub, Addan, *and* Immer: but they could not shew their father's house, and their seed, whether they *were* of Israel: The children of Delaiah, the children of Tobiah, the children of Nekoda, six hundred fifty and two. And of the children of the priests: the children of Habaiah, the children of Koz, the children of Barzillai; which took a wife of the daughters of Barzillai the Gileadite, and was called after their name: These sought their register *among* those that were reckoned by genealogy, but they were not found: therefore were they, as polluted, put from the priesthood" (Ezra 2:59–62).

In the process of the re-establishment of Israel as a nation, the priestly order was once again screened with a fine-toothed comb to secure only those who, by virtue of their lineage, were qualified to engage in the office of the priesthood (see Neh. 10:37–39; 12:47). "The first qualification for the priesthood was descent from Aaron. Genealogical registers were kept with great care (2 Chron. 31:16–19). One who could not submit legal proof of Aaronic descent was not permitted to minister in the priest's office (Ezra 2:62; Neh. 7:64)."[48]

One would think that the trag-edies suffered by Miriam and by Korah, Dathan, and Abiram, the consuming of the 250 princes with fire, and the thousands who were struck dead by a plague because they continued in the impugning rebellion would have made the

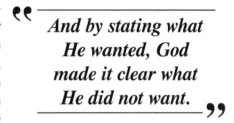

And by stating what He wanted, God made it clear what He did not want.

issue clear. And, if that were not enough, there was also the plague on the thousands that was halted by Aaron's stepping in with his censer as a priest and the subsequent test of the rods giving proof of Aaron's author-ity since his rod was the only one that budded. These should have been conclusive evidence to crush any challenge to the singular choice of Aaron and his sons. This divine election excluded his daughters and his son's daughters as a perpetual mandate for ever.

None of God's followers had any question or doubts as to what God intended. And by stating what He wanted, God made it clear what He did not want. So, if the Lord's people know what He wants, does He need to spell out what He doesn't want? Or is it sufficient to understand by His positive assertion what He has ordained?

48 *The Seventh-day Adventist Bible Commentary*, vol. 1, p. 743, 744, commentary on Leviticus 8:2.

7.

The Priesthood of Believers

The phrase "the priesthood of believers," which declares that all believers are now all priests, surfaces when the issue of ordaining women is being agitated. While it sounds kosher, is it even biblical? I did a search throughout the Bible to find this phrase. Here is what I discovered. First, I could not find it either in the Old Testament or in the New. Since it is not a biblical term, what is its origin? It turns out that it is a borrowed coined phrase suggested to have biblical roots by some. Second, I was able to trace it to the fifteen century Protestant reformer Martin Luther. And, although it is true that he coined and used the phrase, its definition had a different slant than that used today. It was to contradict the Catholic dogma and practice that only the clergy or priests could exclusively approach God. He argued that a common individual was just as capable as a priest to approach God and pray directly to Him. Hence, "the priesthood of all believers." Meaning that every believer has direct access to God.

And while Martin Luther strongly believed in this concept, his practice demonstrates that he did not believe that everyone was a minister or a pastor. His denomination has an order of clergy who lead the church. "Like most mainline Protestant churches, Lutherans have ministers rather than priests. Priests, by definition, are an intermediary between people and the divine. So, for example, in some religions people are required to offer sacrifices to God or the gods, but they are not themselves able to do so and therefore must obtain the services of a priest to sacrifice for them. Martin Luther believed in the priesthood of all believers. In other words, salvation is a gift given directly by God to people, and requires no intermediary. Everyone stands directly before God at judgment, and it would do no good to bring your priest with you."[49]

It is biblically incongruous to form or establish a Scriptural doctrine with one text alone. Nevertheless, in order to promote the idea that all believers are priests, legitimacy and credibility has been gained in the

---

49 "Leadership," https://1ref.us/1uw, accessed 8/22/2021.

minds of some through a single text in the Bible. Yet, the question is: Does this text actually support the concept. Let's see. The text in question is: "Ye also, as lively stones, are built up a spiritual house, an holy priesthood, to offer up spiritual sacrifices, acceptable to God by Jesus Christ. But ye *are* a chosen generation, a royal priesthood, an holy nation, a peculiar people; that ye should shew forth the praises of him who hath called you out of darkness into his marvellous light" (1 Peter 2:5, 9). Question: Did God sweep away the distinction between the believers and the ministry after the cross? Did every believer in the apostolic period become an apostle, an elder, or a pastor?

> *Did God sweep away the distinction between the believers and the ministry after the cross?*

Peter is led by the Spirit to cross-reference this verse from the Old Testament where God said to Israel: "And ye shall be unto me a kingdom of priests, and an holy nation. These *are* the words which thou shalt speak unto the children of Israel" (Exod. 19:6). In Deuteronomy, God restated Israel's elevated status: "And to make thee high above all nations which he hath made, in praise, and in name, and in honour; and that thou mayest be an holy people unto the LORD thy God, as he hath spoken" (Deut. 26:19). What did God mean by this proclamation? Did He intend that everybody in Israel—that adults and children and both males and females should become priests? Obviously, not! What did Moses understand concerning the declaration?

When the Lord told Moses to convey what He had said to Israel, the record states: "And Moses came and called for the elders of the people, and laid before their faces all these words which the LORD commanded him" (Exod. 19:7). Moses did not call the people to inform the men, women, and children of their new role in Israel. No, he only called the male leaders—the elders—to tell them what God had just told him.

The next question is: What did God intend for the makeup of the priesthood to be? How would He demonstrate or make concrete the interpretation of this declaration?

The Lord rendered the interpretation of this declaration when He said: "And thou shalt put upon Aaron the holy garments, and anoint him, and sanctify him; that he may minister unto me in the priest's office. And thou shalt bring his sons, and clothe them with coats: And thou shalt anoint them, as thou didst anoint their father, that they may minister unto me in the priest's office: for their anointing shall surely be an everlasting priesthood throughout their generations" (Exod. 40:13–15). In the New Testament, we find an apostolic commentary by Paul concerning the priesthood: "And verily they that are of the sons of Levi, who receive the office of the priesthood, have a commandment to take tithes of the people according to the law, that is, of their brethren, though they come out of the loins of Abraham" (Heb. 7:5).

It is essential to notice that God himself gave the interpretation and meaning of the statement. It is therefore not subject to doubt or conjecture concerning His will. By setting up the tabernacle and its services and then assigning only Aaron and his sons to serve as priests, God speaks loud and clear, giving a concrete interpretation of the meaning of the proclamation, "a kingdom of priests, a holy nation." God's divine will as revealed is cogent. His intention was that He would govern the entire nation through a holy priesthood. "And to make thee high above all nations which he hath made, in praise, and in name, and in honour; and that thou mayest be an holy people unto the LORD thy God, as he hath spoken" (Deut. 26:19).

When Korah, Dathan, and Abiram rebelled against Moses, the argument they used is precisely the argument that is made today—that "everyone is now a priest." Notice their rationale for their contention. "And they rose up before Moses, with certain of the children of Israel, two hundred and fifty princes of the assembly, famous in the congregation, men of renown: And they gathered themselves together against Moses and against Aaron, and said unto them, *Ye take* too much upon you, seeing all the congregation *are* holy, every one of them, and the LORD *is* among them: wherefore then lift ye up yourselves above the congregation of the LORD" (Num. 16:2, 3)? They were adamant that "every one of them" "is holy." This language suggests that Korah was paraphrasing the statement God made when He called Israel a "holy nation." However, it is interesting that even Korah made the application exclusively to men as priests. And while he is claiming the rights for all the nation, only two hundred and fifty men show up with their censers. And furthermore, while his act was partially correct on the gender, it amounted to a complete rejection of the exclusiveness that God had established.

Another point concerning Korah and his followers is that he also argued that Moses was lifting himself up above the congregation. They were correct in saying that Moses was above the congregation. However, it was not Moses but God who placed him there. Nonetheless, it is the case that to whom much is given much is required. As in a family, community, or nation, there can only be one leader at a time. So it was with God's people. Not everyone had been called to be priests. God had made His selection. And when some chided against Moses and the priests claimed to be advocates for the holiness of the people, in reality they were rebelling against God. Neither Aaron nor Moses urged themselves into their elevated status. It was by God's election. Paul wrote: "And no man taketh this honour unto himself, but he that is called of God, as *was* Aaron. So also Christ glorified not himself to be made an high priest; but he that said unto him, Thou art my Son, today have I begotten thee" (Heb. 5:4, 5). Once more, as he did when writing to Timothy, Paul here states: "No man takes this honor." However, in the book of Timothy, he wrote, "If any man desire the office of a Bishop" (1 Tim. 3:1). This language clarifies that the office of a bishop is a unique, desirable calling that is not held by just anybody. Also, the language also precludes women either taking or desiring the priesthood, for the qualification of being the "husband of one wife" can only be met by a male aspirant.

What then did Peter mean? It was a transparent practice both in Old Testament and New Testament times to address the family and nation by its leaders. In the fall of Adam and Eve, God held Adam responsible. He was the head of the family. (See Gen. 3:16–21.) And while the Hebrew word *"Adam"* can mean "man" or "mankind," the context here makes it plain that God is speaking about the man Adam. After the fall, God said: "Behold the man is become as one of us, to know good and evil: and now, lest he put forth his hand, and take also of the tree of life, and eat, and live for ever: therefore the Lord God sent him forth from the garden of Eden, to till the ground from whence he was taken. So he drove out the man; and he placed at the east of the garden of Eden Cherubims, and a flaming sword which turned every way to keep the way of the tree of life" (Gen. 3:22–24). Take special note that God does not say, "Behold the man and the woman," but rather, "Behold the man!" The evidence is irrefutable that God held and still holds the man responsible for the spiritual wellbeing of the family. The same was true of the church and the nation.

When Peter wrote the "scattered strangers," he was using the same avenue of communication as used by the other apostles who wrote the believers in those days. He sent the message through "Silvanus, a faithful brother" from the *church that is* at Babylon" (1 Peter 5:12, 13). Notice that the subject matter in chapter 2 of Peter's epistle is addressing the believers in general, but he channeled his counsels through godly male leaders. In verse 19 of chapter 2, Peter says, "For this *is* thankworthy, if a man for conscience toward God endure grief, suffering wrongfully."

In chapter 3, Peter splits his counsel, addressing wives in particular and then husbands. Then, in chapter 4, he returns to the body of believers, addressing the congregants through the men. "And above all things have fervent charity among yourselves: for charity shall cover the multitude of sins. Use hospitality one to another without grudging. As every man hath received the gift, *even so* minister the same one to another, as good stewards of the manifold grace of God. If any man speak, *let him speak* as the oracles of God; if any man minister, *let him do it* as of the ability which God giveth: that God in all things may be glorified through Jesus Christ, to whom be praise and dominion for ever and ever. Amen. Beloved, think it not strange concerning the fiery trial which is to try you, as though some strange thing happened unto you: But rejoice, inasmuch as ye are partakers of Christ's sufferings; that, when his glory shall be revealed, ye may be glad also with exceeding joy. If ye be reproached for the name of Christ, happy *are* ye; for the spirit of glory and of God resteth upon you: on their part he is evil spoken of, but on your part he is glorified. But let none of you suffer as a murderer, or *as* a thief, or *as* an evildoer, or as a busybody in other men's matters. Yet if *any man suffer* as a Christian, let him not be ashamed; but let him glorify God on this behalf" (1 Peter 4:8–16).

It would have been highly unlikely for the apostles to bypass the men or elders of the church and write to the wives or women to give advice to the men. That is why he wrote in chapter 5, "The elders which are among you I exhort, who am also an elder, and a witness of the sufferings of Christ, and also a partaker of the glory that shall be revealed" (1 Peter 5:1). It is only the apostle John who wrote a personal pastoral letter, which is inserted in the Bible, to the "elect lady." (See 2 John.) Otherwise, all counsels sent to the churches were sent to the elders or leaders and read by them to the churches. These church leaders were all men. In fact, the very title "bishop" is always applied to the male gender and never to women.

The apostle Paul also followed the same practice when writing to the churches. To the Corinthian believers—through their male leaders—he wrote: "I write not these things to shame you, but as my beloved sons I warn *you*" (1 Cor. 4:14). In chapter 10, verse 15, he further wrote, "I speak as to wise men; judge ye what I say." Then he admonished them: "Watch ye, stand fast in the faith, quit you like men, be strong" (1 Cor. 16:13). Oftentimes, when addressing the churches, he refers to the leaders with the endearing term "brethren." While today this term is sometimes used for all believers, in the Bible, it refers to males considered to be blood relatives or to male believers. Notice: "And Jesus, walking by the sea of Galilee, saw two brethren, Simon called Peter, and Andrew his brother, casting a net into the sea: for they were fishers. ... And going on from thence, he saw other two brethren, James *the son* of Zebedee, and John his brother, in a ship with Zebedee their father, mending their nets; and he called them" (Matt. 4:18, 21). Today, we would say, "two brothers," while, in the time of the King James translators, they said, "two brethren." Clearly, Paul is holding the men responsible for their families and the believers, as God did in the Old Testament. Moses wrote: "Only take heed to thyself, and keep thy soul diligently, lest thou forget the things which thine eyes have seen, and lest they depart from thy heart all the days of thy life: but teach them thy sons, and thy sons' sons" (Deut. 4:9).

James, the leader of the New Testament church, recommended that sick believers not call for just anyone to anoint the sick but that the sick call for the elders to anoint them (James 5:13–15). The elders were vested with certain responsibilities to use the specific gifts granted them by the Holy Spirit in accordance with their high calling. This is why Paul was led to write out the qualifications necessary for a man to fill the position of a church leader. He wrote: "This *is* a true saying, If a man desire the office of a bishop, he desireth a good work. A bishop then must be blameless, the husband of one wife, vigilant, sober, of good behaviour, given to hospitality, apt to teach" (1 Tim. 3:1, 2). "For a bishop must be blameless, as the steward of God; not selfwilled, not soon angry, not given to wine, no striker, not given to filthy lucre; But a lover of hospitality, a lover of good men, sober, just, holy, temperate; Holding fast the faithful word as he hath been taught, that he may be able by sound doctrine both to exhort and to convince the gainsayers" (Titus 1:7–9). This title used for Christ by Peter is analogously transferred to human undershepherds. "For ye were as sheep going astray; but are now returned unto the Shepherd and Bishop of your souls" (1 Peter 2:25).

The words "elders" and "elder" are generally used as a title for the men who lead out in the Christian church. The word "elder" is used only once as an adjective in contrasting young women from elderly women. In this instance, Paul used the word first as a noun and then as an adjective, Paul wrote: "Rebuke not an elder, but entreat *him* as a father; *and* the younger men as brethren; the elder women as mothers; the younger as sisters, with all purity" (1 Tim. 5:1, 2). Regarding women, he is using the word in respect to age contrasting the older women with the younger ones. But all the rest of the time, he used the word to refer to the male leaders of God's church. For example: "And from Miletus he sent to Ephesus, and called the elders of the church. And when they were come to him, he said unto them, Ye know, from the first day that I came into Asia, after what manner I have been with you at all seasons" (Acts 20:17, 18).

That Paul recognized the existence of duly authorized church leadership is clear. When instructing Timothy about the spiritual authority vested in the leadership, he wrote: "These things command and teach. Let no man despise thy youth; but be thou an example of the believers, in word, in conversation, in charity, in spirit, in faith, in purity. Till I come, give attendance to reading, to exhortation, to doctrine. Neglect not the gift that is in thee, which was given thee by prophecy, with the laying on of the hands of the presbytery" (1 Tim. 4:11–14). The word "presbytery," comes from the Greek *presbuterion*, which means "body of elders, presbytery, senate, council—

1a) of the Jewish elders

1b) of the elders of any body (assembly) of Christians."[50]

Another word describing leadership in the church is "bishop." Strong's Greek Dictionary of the New Testament defines "bishop," or *episkopos* (Strong's #1985), as an "overseer," which is—

1a) a man charged with the duty of seeing that things to be done by others are done rightly, any curator, guardian or superintendent

1b) the superintendent, elder, or overseer of a Christian church.[51]

50 "Presbuterion," at https://1ref.us/1ux, accessed 12/9/21.
51 "Episkopos," at https://1ref.us/1uy, accessed 12/9/21.

It is plain to see that the term "elders" was used among Christians as "those who presided over the assemblies (or churches). The New Testament uses the term bishop, elders, and presbyters interchangeably."[52]

Paul wrote in the succeeding verses: "Against an elder receive not an accusation, but before two or three witnesses. Them that sin rebuke before all, that others also may fear. I charge *thee* before God, and the Lord Jesus Christ, and the elect angels, that thou observe these things without preferring one before another, doing nothing by partiality. Lay hands suddenly on no man, neither be partaker of other men's sins: keep thyself pure" (1 Tim. 5:19–22). Take special note that he did not write: "lay hands suddenly on no *woman*," but rather on "no *man*."

The conclusion of this matter is that Peter is using a declaration and analogy from the Old Testament. James wrote to the believers in his day: "James, a servant of God and the Lord Jesus Christ, to the twelve tribes which are scattered abroad, greetings" (James 1:1). And James' brother Jude, admonishing the believers, wrote: "Jude, the servant of Jesus Christ, and brother of James, to them that are sanctified by God the Father, and preserved in Jesus Christ, and called" (Jude 1:1). Peter and the other apostles recognized the New Testament church as the replacement of the Old Testament church, which is why they addressed all believers as "the Israel of God." Peter intended to convey the reality that just as God had chosen Israel to function as a nation under the spiritual leadership of a priesthood (which was made up of males) under God's guidance, so also should the Jewish and gentile believers see themselves as a chosen people functioning in the same relationship with God that ancient Israel enjoyed. This was in contrast to other nations In other words, as the priests offered sacrifices in the Old Testament and led in the spiritual matters of Israel, so, in the same sense, should God's New Testament church leaders hold sacred the spiritual responsibilities of the churches, and every member should live a holy life in the same way that He intended that Israel of old should live.

In the New Testament, the title of the leaders was changed from "priest," to "elder" or "pastor." Also, the offering in the New Testament was no longer to be a dying animal but rather the dying and risen Lamb, Jesus Christ. The change of title suggested that the Old Testament sacrifices and offerings had ceased, giving way to the heavenly priesthood of Christ and creating a new order. Paul makes

---

52 "Elders," Strong's Analytical Lexicon at https://1ref.us/1uz, accessed 12/9/21.

it clear that God's New Testament church would be led by the High Priest Christ Jesus. He wrote: "Wherefore, holy brethren, partakers of the heavenly calling, consider the Apostle and High Priest of our profession, Christ Jesus; ... For every high priest taken from among men is ordained for men in things *pertaining* to God, that he may offer both gifts and sacrifices for sins: Who can have compassion on the ignorant, and on them that are out of the way; for that he himself also is compassed with infirmity. And by reason hereof he ought, as for the people, so also for himself, to offer for sins. And no man taketh this honour unto himself, but he that is called of God, as *was* Aaron. So also Christ glorified not himself to be made an high priest; but he that said unto him, Thou art my Son, to day have I begotten thee" (Heb. 3:1; 5:1–5). God would be their God, leading a holy church with leaders as in times past. However, the church would no longer be led by earthly priests from Aaron's line but, rather, by the heavenly Priest, Christ Jesus, with elders, or pastors, under Him.

This new order is underscored by Peter when he wrote: "The elders which are among you I exhort, who am also an elder, and a witness of the sufferings of Christ, and also a partaker of the glory that shall be revealed: Feed the flock of God which is among you, taking the oversight *thereof*, not by constraint, but willingly; not for filthy lucre, but of a ready mind; Neither as being lords over *God's* heritage, but being ensamples to the flock. And when the chief Shepherd shall appear, ye shall receive a crown of glory that fadeth not away" (1 Peter 5:1–4). Paul also made the same distinction between the leadership and the followers. To the believers in Thessalonians he wrote: "And we beseech you, brethren, to know them which labour among you, and are over you in the Lord, and admonish you; And to esteem them very highly in love for their work's sake. *And* be at peace among yourselves" (1 Thess. 5:12, 13). Then to the leaders he admonished, "Now we exhort you, brethren, warn them that are unruly, comfort the feebleminded, support the weak, be patient toward all *men*" (verse 14). Then solemnly charging the leaders, he added, "I charge you by the Lord that this epistle be read unto all the holy brethren" (verses 27). To the Hebrew believers Paul wrote, "Remember them which have the rule over you, who have spoken unto you the word of God: whose faith follow, considering the end of *their* conversation. ... Obey them that have the rule over you, and submit yourselves: for they watch for your souls, as they that must give account, that they may do it with joy, and not with grief: for that *is* unprofitable for you. ... Salute all them that have the rule over you, and all the saints. They of Italy salute you" (Heb. 13:7, 17, 24).

Yes, thank God the spiritual status proclaimed over ancient Israel has been transferred to the New Testament Christian church, for the church is now a "holy nation" under a "royal priesthood." Today spiritual Israel is God's holy people as led by godly men under the direct leadership of our High Priest Jesus Christ.

8.

Ministry
Calling or Career,
Ordination or Commissioning

One of my first tasks in the work of ministry was to train pastors and laity in practical aspects of soul winning. The president of the conference requested that I go to southern Maryland to help a pastor in a certain district. Upon my arrival, I first sought to get acquainted with the man to determine the particular areas that he felt he needed help with. I found that the pastor was well equipped with his education, having earned a Master of Divinity degree. But, while he was well educated, he felt a lack in the practical areas of ministry. This confirmed the reason for the president sending me to help him.

As soon as he was ready, I took him out to demonstrate the different ways to make contact with people and the way to determine whether or not a person was a potential candidate for Bible studies. I demonstrated approaches on the street, at the supermarket, and in door-to-door contacts. After spending two days with him with good success, I let him know that I needed to return home and would be back the following day to see how he had soloed.

"Nothing doing!" He retorted, "I am not going out by myself."

"What do you mean?" I questioned. "My career is on the line. The president is coming here to do an evangelistic series of meetings, and I am not going to sink alone. If I sink, you are going to sink with me!"

I was surprised and saddened. Surprised, that is, because I never thought of ministry as a career but, rather, as a calling, and saddened, because this pastor had a terrible opinion of his president and little confidence in the capability of his own calling—that of a soul winner. So, is ministry a job, or is it a calling?

The first mention in Holy Writ of the work of ministry is of Abel, Adam's son. He is introduced as offering the sacrificial lamb. After his untimely demise, his brother Seth took up the solemn task of keeping the

Lord before others. "And Adam knew his wife again; and she bare a son, and called his name Seth: For God, said she, hath appointed me another seed instead of Abel, whom Cain slew. And to Seth, to him also there was born a son; and he called his name Enos: then began men to call upon the name of the LORD" (Gen. 4:25, 26). Enoch is mentioned, and it is by obvious divine election that he did the work of preaching. "And Enoch also, the seventh from Adam, prophesied of these, saying, Behold, the Lord cometh with ten thousands of his saints, To execute judgment upon all, and to convince all that are ungodly among them of all their ungodly deeds which they have ungodly committed, and of all their hard *speeches* which ungodly sinners have spoken against him" (Jude 1:14, 15).

Though not specifically stated, the evidence is obvious that these men were selected by God to carry out His work. For at least two thousand plus years, from the creation of mankind until the time of the flood, ten patriarchs are named. The list includes Adam, Seth, Enos, Cainan, Mahalaleel, Jared, Enoch, Methuselah, Lamech (Genesis, chapter 5), and ends with God calling Noah (Gen. 6:8–18). From among the multitudes that were living in those days, he was chosen to declare the message to be given to the antediluvians. "And he [Lamech] called his name Noah, saying, This *same* shall comfort us concerning our work and toil of our hands, because of the ground which the LORD hath cursed. And Lamech lived after he begat Noah five hundred ninety and five years, and begat sons and daughters" (Gen. 5:29, 30). After the flood, Noah gave evidence of his spiritual role by offering sacrifice. Except for Enoch, all of these men lived out their calling, terminating in death.

After Noah, the Lord called Abraham (Gen. 12:1–3). As the father of the faithful, he was God's representative (Genesis 20) and was faithful to his calling until he died (Gen. 25:7, 8). The torch was then passed to Isaac, and the Lord declared: "My covenant will I establish with Isaac, which Sarah shall bear unto thee at this set time in the next year" (Gen. 17:21). And like his father Abraham, Isaac also terminated his calling in death. Once more, the divine line of the chosen was passed on to Jacob (Gen. 25:23; 48:3), who, in turn, continued his calling until his death (Gen. 49:33). None of these men, though feeble and sinful, considered their calling a job, or a career to retire from. God then selected from Jacob's loins a priesthood through the tribe of Levi—the Aaronic priesthood (Exod. 28:1)—which, by divine appointment, would likewise terminate in death (Num. 35:25–32). "And Moses stripped Aaron of his garments, and put them upon Eleazar his son; and Aaron died there in the top of the mount: and Moses and Eleazar came down from the mount" (Num. 20:28).

There is no record in the Old Testament of anyone called by God to serve Him being released from their calling by anything but death. This includes priests, prophets, judges, and kings. All, whether faithful or unfaithful, like Aaron's unfaithful sons (Num. 26:61) or a wicked king like Ahab (1 Kings 16:30; 22:40), terminated their appointment at death. This is also true in the New Testament. All the chosen apostles of Christ, including Paul, considered their calling to be of divine origin, and none considered their calling a career or just a job. Paul wrote, "And no man taketh this honour unto himself, but he that is called of God, as was Aaron" (Heb. 5:4). And, as it was true of those in the Old Testament, so was it true in the New Testament that all those who were called ended their ministry at death. Again, Paul wrote to the Corinthians, "Paul, an Apostle of Jesus Christ by the will of God ... Now he which stablisheth us with you in Christ, and hath anointed us, is God" (2 Cor. 1:1, 22).

The reality is that men are called not to a career but to a lifelong service of ministry. And, inasmuch as this is the biblical case, there must be a Scriptural public certification, evidence, or recognition of that calling. This certification the Bible calls "anointing." Today we call it ordination. From the Bible we know that Aaron was anointed, and so were his sons. Elisha was called to ministry and anointed. "And Jehu the son of Nimshi shalt thou anoint *to be* king over Israel: and Elisha the son of Shaphat of Abelmeholah shalt thou anoint *to be* prophet in thy room" (1 King 19:16). And, while it may not be mentioned in every case, it is a known fact that all who served in ministry in the Old Testament were ordained by either anointing or the laying on of hands or both. For example, "Elisha the prophet called one of the children of the prophets, and said unto him, Gird up thy loins, and take this box of oil in thine hand, and go to Ramothgilead: And when thou comest thither, look out there Jehu the son of Jehoshaphat the son of Nimshi, and go in, and make him arise up from among his brethren, and carry him to an inner chamber; Then take the box of oil, and pour *it* on his head, and say, Thus saith the LORD, I have anointed thee king over Israel. Then open the door, and flee, and tarry not. So the young man, *even* the young man the prophet, went to Ramothgilead. And when he came, behold, the captains of the host *were* sitting; and he said, I have an errand to thee, O captain. And Jehu said, Unto which of all us? And he said, To thee, O captain. And he arose, and went into the house; and he poured the oil on his head, and said unto him,

Thus saith the LORD God of Israel, I have anointed thee king over the people of the LORD, *even* over Israel" (2 Kings 9:1–6). While this record confirms Jehu's anointing, there is no such record for Elisha. Yet, it is clear that his last act of ministry was to the young visiting king, prior to his death. "And he said, Take the arrows. And he took *them*. And he said unto the king of Israel, Smite upon the ground. And he smote thrice, and stayed. And the man of God was wroth with him, and said, Thou shouldest have smitten five or six times; then hadst thou smitten Syria till thou hadst consumed *it*: whereas now thou shalt smite Syria *but* thrice. And Elisha died, and they buried him" (2 Kings 13:18–20). From his youth, Elisha faithfully fulfilled his calling and performed the duties of his office until this final act of ministry saw his parting breath.

In the New Testament, the same is true. Men were called and set apart. Yet, unlike the practice in the Old Testament, rather than anointing with oil, in the New Testament, the laying on of hands was the chosen method of ordination. Perhaps the reason for the laying on of hands, is because, in the Old Testament, the oil was a symbol of the Holy Ghost, while, in the New Testament, men were given the Holy Ghost by means of the laying on of hands. "Then laid they *their* hands on them, and they received the Holy Ghost" (Acts 8:17). Paul wrote to Timothy: "Neglect not the gift that is in thee, which was given thee by prophecy, with the laying on of the hands of the presbytery" (1 Tim. 4:14).

That was yesterday, and unfortunately, yesterday is gone. A new way of setting men apart that would be inclusive of women in some places is no longer ordination, but rather something called "commissioning." Who ordained this new mode? Certainly not the Lord, for there is no record of God ordering a change in His Word. Where then did it come from and why? The first time I heard the word "commissioning" was in my adolescence while watching movies, when ships were commissioned to war by breaking a bottle of champaign. Later, my wife was concert master of the Long Island Symphony under Maestro Laszlo Halasz, who was "commissioned" by the United States government to make a recording of Christmas songs from around the world.

I personally became entangled with the word as I was serving as the Executive Secretary of the Greater New York Conference in New York City. Normally speaking, it used to be when men entered into the ministry of the church that they began as unordained workers. After four or five years, depending on the level of their education, with either a Master of Divinity or a Bachelor of Arts, the person who demonstrated a calling to ministry, as evidenced by the level of his work of mission and service, could be ordained. As soon as the individual was ordained, his salary went up. At the same time, those who had worked for years as a school principal, superintendent of education, or conference treasurer were surpassed in remuneration by such newly ordained individuals.

This became an issue. Those who had served longer felt it an injustice to be remunerated less simply because they were not on the "ordination track." Because it became a major problem, the need arose to address the matter and rectify the inequity. Hence, "commissioning" was the term chosen to describe those not on the ordination track. Along with the term, a special service was created to highlight the elevation of status for the persons thus commissioned. But what does the word actually mean? This is what I found on the Internet: "To commission is to charge someone with a task, giving them the authority to do something in an official way. The gerund form of the verb, commissioning, can be used as a noun referring to the action of authorizing someone or something."

This new mode of setting a person apart for ministry in some quarters has become a substitute for ordination because of the issue of women in the pastoral role. Inasmuch as the world church refused to sanction the ordination of women on what it felt were biblical grounds, factions within the church against the church's official position determined to get women into the pastoral role without the world church's approval. Based on one professor's declaration that ordination was Catholic and not biblical, they discarded ordination as a "Catholic dogma." In place of ordination, commissioning was instituted. Thus, a secular non-biblical and man-made ordinance became the way to set apart men for sacred ministry. It's curious that, for the sake of placing women in pastoral roles, men in some places are no longer able to follow the biblical rite of being set apart for a holy purpose. Strange!

It may seem enigmatic that something as sacred as a call from God to serve Him no longer qualifies for ordination. Instead, it is downgraded to a secular level of getting a man-made command to do a holy service. This is incongruent! Having a commissioning service to set apart a man for the ministry is an oxymoron.

I was saddened when a young man wrote me to share a picture of his "commissioning" to the ministry. "This was done," he said, "because the leadership no longer believes that ordination is biblical." He felt that he was being forced to accept this unbiblical mode in order to follow what he considered to be God's calling into ministry. Well did the prophet record the words of God: "Her priests have violated my law, and have profaned mine holy things: they have put no difference between the holy and profane, neither have they shewed *difference* between the unclean and the clean, and have hid their eyes from my sabbaths, and I am profaned among them" (Ezek. 22:26).

> *Is God still calling men to the ministry or are men calling men to the ministry?*

The question to those who have abandoned ordination in exchange for commissioning is this: Is *God* still calling men to the ministry or are *men* calling men to the ministry? If it is God, then shouldn't ordination, as described in Scripture, be the authentic means of recognizing His calling? This question should provoke grave concerns as to the direction that the pro-women ordination issue is heading. Consider the falling away of ancient Israel as they began to make no difference between what God considered holy and what He considered common. This anti-ordination ordinance is doing the same thing that took place with baptism by immersion. Rather than follow the mode exemplified by Christ, some have chosen to abandon it and replace it with christening. Thus, they have substituted unbiblical humanly-devised practices for God's sacred ordinances.

In some parts of the country the emblems of the Lord's Supper are now being substituted by pizza and soda pop. Unto what ends will this lead? Can men indeed have the authority to change what God has ordained? Or, by the changes, is it possible that men are inadvertently setting themselves up above the Creator?

9.

The Holy and the Profane

In the previous chapter, we noted a very important text regarding the holy and the profane. Let's look at that text again. "Her priests have violated my law, and have profaned mine holy things: they have put no difference between the holy and profane" (Ezek. 22:26). God intended that there be no ambiguity between the two. This separation is clearly set forth from the very beginning. God's declaration that the seventh day was holy was intentional. It was the introduction of distinctiveness, an implied and yet clear invitation to holiness—the revelation of that which God declared holy. Of all things inanimate and animate mentioned in the creation week—the stars, the sun, the moon, water, trees, plants, breath, and days—only one thing was placed above all others and "hallowed." It was the Sabbath. By inference, God intended that mankind share this hallowed time where only holiness could coexist.

It was not until Eve wandered away from Adam that the elevated position that God had intended for our first parents was challenged as insufficient for man's happiness. That which was holy was subjugated, or relegated to a common ground. The statement, "Yea, hath God said, Ye shall not eat of every tree of the garden?" (Gen. 3:1) was intended to challenge what God had spoken. If Satan the deceiver was to gain a foothold in the creation, it would have to be by means of downgrading and substituting that which God had said, making superior what Satan suggested. Once the objective was gained, the holy status of mankind plummeted in the dust.

The first afront to the sanctity of God's faith was the sanctimonious offering of Cain in contrast to the reverent offering of his brother Abel, whom Cain slew. Why did Cain kill Abel? "Because his own works were evil, and his brother's righteous" (1 John 3:12). After Abel's death, God provided a replacement—Seth. Seth's birth and life elevated the distinction of the holy from the common and once more established holiness. "And Adam knew his wife again; and she bare a son, and called his name Seth: For God, *said she*, hath appointed me another seed instead of Abel, whom Cain slew. And to Seth, to him also there was born a son; and he called his name Enos: then began men to call upon the name of the LORD" (Gen. 4:25, 26). Through Seth's line, God was able to maintain the distinction of holiness in contrast to Cain's line.

Tragically, though, the distinctiveness was nearly obliterated with the amalgamation of the Sethites with the Cainites. "And it came to pass, when men began to multiply on the face of the earth, and daughters were born unto them, That the sons of God saw the daughters of men that they *were* fair; and they took them wives of all which they chose. And the LORD said, My spirit shall not always strive with man, for that he also *is* flesh: yet his days shall be an hundred and twenty years. There were giants in the earth in those days; and also after that, when the sons of God came in unto the daughters of men, and they bare *children* to them, the same *became* mighty men which *were* of old, men of renown" (Gen. 6:1–4).

From all the righteous line of Seth, by the time of the impending doom, there remained only eight persons—Noah, his sons, and all their wives (Gen. 7:13). So, for the sake of preserving the human race, God quarantined the faithful, destroyed the wicked, and replanted the saints to replenish the earth (Matt. 13:38, 39; 24:38, 39). In reference to the baleful evil consequences of the mixture of the sons of God (Sethites) with the daughters of men (Cainites), Paul was later inspired to write: "Be ye not unequally yoked together with unbelievers: for what fellowship hath righteousness with unrighteousness? and what communion hath light with darkness? And what concord hath Christ with Belial? or what part hath he that believeth with an infidel? And what agreement hath the temple of God with idols? for ye are the temple of the living God; as God hath said, I will dwell in them, and walk in *them*; and I will be their God, and they shall be my people. Wherefore come out from among them, and be ye separate, saith the Lord, and touch not the unclean *thing;* and I will receive you, And will be a Father unto you, and ye shall be my sons and daughters, saith the Lord Almighty" (2 Cor. 6:14–18).

Moving forward from the time of Noah, we find another parting of ways between the righteous and the unrighteous. Like Cain, Ham departed from the path of holiness and became the progenitor of all the pagan religions (Gen. 10:6–20; Ps. 105:23, 27). Once more it appeared that Satan's influence in leading mankind to depart from holiness was accomplishing his goal of ridding God from men. Satan knew that without holiness "no man shall see the Lord" (Heb. 12:14). Thankfully, Abraham appears on the scene as the father of the faithful, keeping a distinction between the holy and the profane, and, through him, the religion of God was kept alive. "Because that Abraham obeyed my voice, and kept my charge, my commandments, my statutes, and my laws" (Gen. 26:5). His faith was passed on to Isaac and then on to Jacob and then on to the twelve patriarchs, which were relocated to Egypt by Joseph during the great famine (Acts 7:11–17).

Then, for approximately 400 plus years (Gen. 15:13; Acts 7:17), the enemy of souls sought to eliminate God's people, and, by so doing, destroy the distinctive elements of a holy faith. But God would not allow that. In mercy He protected the child Moses, and, through him, brought out His people from the center of idolatry to re-establish the holy faith that saves.

When the devil lost the battle in the stronghold of idolatry in Egypt, he sought for ways to destroy the true faith, though, this time, not by a genocide but by amalgamating the holy with the profane. He knew that the mixture of the two would completely render the gospel powerless. The terrifying thing about what happened with the Hebrews and the golden calf is that it was the high priest Aaron who encouraged and participated in the spiritual fusing of truth and error, of the sacred and the abominable. Terrible was the outcome of this adulterous service under the guise of worshiping God through an idol. (See Exod. 32:1–28.) When profession is negated by actions, religion becomes a deadly pluralistic poison to spirituality.

To counteract the subversive elements of this attack, God eradicated anything that countenanced paganism by setting up the true worship system. God said, "And let them make me a sanctuary; that I may dwell among them" (Exod. 25:8). The Lord intended to transform slaves into a holy nation. Everything from their clothing to their food, from their health and sanitary practices to their dwellings, were all to be holy. "For I *am* the LORD that bringeth you up out of the land of Egypt, to be your God: ye shall therefore be holy, for I *am* holy" (Lev. 11:45). From this point forth their standing with God was dependent upon their holding onto that which was holy rather than that which was not. This was their defense against the wiles of the enemy. As long as they kept their connection with the Lord and upheld the distinction between the holy and the profane, Satan could not touch them.

As a holy nation, they were invincible. No one could resist or stand up against them. There was only one way then that Satan could win—that was from within. The first instance of this was with Aaron and the golden calf. The next was with a prophet named Balaam. All of Balaam's efforts to curse Israel failed and attested that the people of Israel had kept themselves within the confines of God's order. Balaam himself said: "Behold, I have received *commandment* to bless: and he hath blessed; and I cannot reverse it. He hath not beheld iniquity in Jacob, neither hath he seen perverseness in Israel: the LORD his God *is* with him, and the shout of a king *is* among them. God brought them out of Egypt; he hath as it were the strength of a unicorn" (Num. 23:20–22). While Balaam (who was apparently recognized as a prophet by the Israelites) could not curse Israel, he used his influence to encourage the Israelites to attend a cultural feast, which had been planned to seduce them into licentiousness and cause their downfall, ending in an alliance that would be disastrous to them. Falling from their holy state, they became a prey to their enemies.

Another of Satan's efforts was to incite, in Israel, a religious coup d'état. Korah and his three friends attempted to obliterate the distinction between the people and the ministry by doing the opposite of what Balaam had done. Rather than leading the people into obvious sin, the devil succeeded in lifting up a revolt against what God had set up as holy— the priesthood. And while the demand for equality may have appeared to be genuinely justifiable, equality turned out to be another attempt of the enemy to disguise his efforts, under the cover of respected leaders of the congregation, to break down the distinction between the sacred and the common. Satan sought to lower the priesthood from its holy distinction by suggesting, in his shrewdness, that all the people were holy, making the common rise to the level of supposed holiness. Common believers (though of high rank) took up censers (considered to be holy), declaring themselves to be priests. But God would not have it. Once, through God's obvious retribution, it became clear that the priesthood pertained only to the select few, no one dared (at least while Moses and Joshua were alive) to keep their shoes on while standing on holy ground, so to speak. The priesthood was holy. Its ministry was only to be carried out by those that God Himself had set apart for it.

The next attack on that which was holy occurred after Israel entered the Holy Land. Firstly, Joshua was to maintain his standing with God by faithfully preserving that which was spiritual. The Lord admonished, "Only be thou strong and very courageous, that thou mayest observe to do according to all the law, which Moses my servant commanded thee: turn not from it *to* the right hand or *to* the left, that thou mayest prosper whithersoever thou goest. This book of the law shall not depart out of thy mouth; but thou shalt meditate therein day and night, that thou mayest observe to do according to all that is written therein: for then thou shalt make thy way prosperous, and then thou shalt have good success" (Joshua 1:7, 8).

Then, God ordered Joshua to lead the people in overthrowing the inhabitants of Jericho. The city would render to Israel the first fruits of the land, for God had commanded: "But all the silver, and gold, and vessels of brass and iron, *are* consecrated unto the LORD: they shall come into the treasury of the LORD" (Joshua 6:19). These metals were devoted as a tithe, which was holy. Once again, the enemy of souls led an Israelite named Achan to make no difference between the holy and the profane. "But the children of Israel committed a trespass in the accursed thing: for Achan, the son of Carmi, the son of Zabdi, the son of Zerah, of the tribe of Judah, took of the accursed thing: and the anger of the LORD was kindled against the children of Israel" (Joshua 7:1). But Achan's betrayal was not discovered until the defeat at Ai. Though God gave time for the guilty party to make things right, Achan's only response, when he was singled out, was to admit that he had taken a "goodly Babylonish garment, and two hundred shekels of silver, and a wedge of gold of fifty shekels weight" (Joshua 7:21). His covetous spirit drove him to rob that which God had commanded to be set apart, and it left his family vulnerable to participating with their father in his rebellious deed. Though the retribution for the deed made an example of Achan, that has not stopped later violations by those who allow the enemy of souls to lead them into the terrible act of mixing the holy with the unholy.

This unholy admixture contributed to the frequent downfall of God's people. While the restitution of a genuine reverence for that which was considered holy by such men as Samuel, Elijah, Elisha, Isaiah, Jeremiah, Nehemiah, Ezra (Neh. 8:5, 6, 8–11), and others was realized, and the elevation of a true regard for what the Word revealed to be sacred was uplifted. There were those like Balaam, Ahab and Jezebel, Jeroboam (1 Kings 12:31, 32), and others that did the opposite. The terrible and sad record states: "Judah hath dealt treacherously, and an abomination is committed in Israel and in Jerusalem; for Judah hath profaned the holiness of the LORD which he loved, and hath married the daughter of a strange god" (Mal. 2:11). Yet, while Israel was sinking in the mire of apostasy, God declared: "But upon mount Zion shall be deliverance, and there shall be holiness; and the house of Jacob shall possess their possessions" (Obadiah 1:17).

Oh, how hard it is for mankind to learn the lesson of differentiating between what God calls or determines to be holy from that which is profane. The examples are many. The Scriptures are replete with violations and their sure consequences—from the sons of Aaron offering common fire on a sacred altar, to Samson's betrayal of the sacred call that was given him, then streaming through time to Eli's sons and their abuses of the priest's office culminating with his death and the death of his dissolute sons (see 1 Sam. 2:17). It was sad that the heathen gave more reverence to the captured ark than those anointed to sacred office. "And the Philistines called for the priests and the diviners, saying, What shall we do to the ark of the LORD? tell us wherewith we shall send it to his place. And they said, If ye send away the ark of the God of Israel, send it not empty; but in any wise return him a trespass offering: then ye shall be healed, and it shall be known to you why his hand is not removed from you" (1 Sam. 6:2, 3).

Kings were not innocent in this matter. The violation of the first king of Israel, Saul, is registered as a stern warning. His anointing as a king did not render him innocent when, in the place of a priest, he offered a sacrifice. God rejected him as king (1 Samuel 16) and eventually the Spirit departed from Saul (1 Sam. 16:14). His final tragic end remains in Holy Writ, as Paul observed: "Now all these things happened unto them for ensamples: and they are written for our admonition, upon whom the ends of the world are come" (1 Cor. 10:11).

Of all the sins committed, the most euphoriant is the illusion of self-deception, which convinces oneself that one is pleasing God, when in reality self is the object. This delusion steps over God and places self on the throne. Casting aside what God ordained as sacred and, in His name, replacing it with something else, is the epitome of idolatry. And, inasmuch as the Holy Scriptures are the only means of revealing God in Christ and His teachings and counsels, which reveal what is and is not acceptable to Him, it becomes transparent why there are ferocious attacks on the Bible. For in them is revealed what is holy and what is profane, "that ye may prove what *is* that good, and acceptable, and perfect, will of God" (Rom. 12:2).

The true religion of God has a unique role and purpose in the life of a human being. It calls him to holiness; it takes a degraded man and lifts him up. It makes him noble and refined; the thoughtless and wayward becomes serious; the licentious becomes pure; the drunkard becomes sober; the obstinate rebel becomes meek and Christlike; the crude and rough becomes kind, tender, and sensitive; the thief becomes honest. All of these elevated characteristics stem from holiness. On the other hand, mere religion without holiness corrupts, degrades, and makes a man twice the "child of hell" (Matt. 23:15) that he was.

The *Seventh-day Adventist Bible Dictionary* defines "holy" as: "The rendering of several closely synonymous Greek and Hebrew words which refer in general to that which is sacred or set apart from the common. Besides connoting a separation from all that defiles, the terms also usually include, when referring to people of God, the concept of moral perfection, and there is often a strong emphasis upon dedication to religious or sacred use (cf. Ex 19:6; 30:31, 32; Lev 21:6; Heb 3:1; etc.). The term appears in: (1) references to the absolute holiness of God (1 Sa 2:2; Ps 99:9; Is 6:3; Rev 15:4; etc.); (2) the expression 'Holy One of Israel,' a title of the Lord (Is 47:4; Eze 39:7; etc.); (3) the names of the compartments of the sanctuary and Temple (Ex 26:33; 2 Chr 4:22; Heb 9:12; etc.); (4) references to the holy character expected of the people of God (1 Pe 1:15, 16); etc."[53] Holiness is the virtue by which one makes all one's acts subservient to God.

Holiness, therefore, is an essential element in the relationship with God. "Without which no man shall see the Lord" (Heb. 12:14). It is a divine attribute passed on to persons desiring godliness, a quality placed on that which God determines to be holy. To Israel He said, "And thou shalt make a plate *of* pure gold, and grave upon it, *like* the engravings of a signet, HOLINESS TO THE LORD" (Exod. 28:36). God held the priests and spiritual leaders responsible for keeping the line of demarcation clear. He declared: "And they shall teach my people *the difference* between the holy and profane, and cause them to discern between the unclean and the clean" (Ezek. 44:23).

To the Roman believers, Paul presents the contrast between both: "I speak after the manner of men because of the infirmity of your flesh: for as ye have yielded your members servants to uncleanness and to iniquity unto iniquity; even so now yield your members servants to righteousness unto holiness. ... But now being made free from sin, and become servants to God, ye have your fruit unto holiness, and the end everlasting life" (Rom. 6:19, 22). He presents holiness not only as something desirable and necessary but as reachable, a concept that today many consider a staggering level to reach and wholly unattainable. And it would be impossible, if it were not for His promises. "Having therefore these promises, dearly

---

53 "Holy," *Seventh-day Adventist Bible Dictionary*, p. 484.

beloved, let us cleanse ourselves from all filthiness of the flesh and spirit, perfecting holiness in the fear of God" (2 Cor. 7:1). "And that ye put on the new man, which after God is created in righteousness and true holiness" (Eph. 4:24). "For God hath not called us unto uncleanness, but unto holiness" (1 Thess. 4:7). The apostle Peter also contributes with: "Whereby are given unto us exceeding great and precious promises: that by these ye might be partakers of the divine nature, having escaped the corruption that is in the world through lust. And beside this, giving all diligence, add to your faith virtue; and to virtue knowledge; And to knowledge temperance; and to temperance patience; and to patience godliness; And to godliness brotherly kindness; and to brotherly kindness charity. For if these things be in you, and abound, they make *you that ye shall* neither *be* barren nor unfruitful in the knowledge of our Lord Jesus Christ" (2 Peter 1:4–8).

The danger is not what we perceive as unreachable—holiness. Rather, the danger is in becoming complacent, lukewarm, and careless with that which God declares holy. The Lord is holy (1 Sam. 2:2); the Bible is holy (Ps. 138:2; Rom. 1:2; 1 Tim. 3:15–17); the Sabbath is holy (Gen. 2:2, 3; Exod. 20:8–11); God's church is holy (Acts 20:20; Eph. 5:27); the ministry is holy (1 Cor. 9:13).

Is it possible that the desire to bring God down to a common level to impress people with His kindness and goodness may rob Him of His rightful position as the Potentate of the universe, worthy of reverence and respect? Could it be that the pendulum is being swung from a horrible portrait of God, vengefully looking to strike people down with lightning for the least offence, to a harmless ever-forgiving portrait of God, holding no one accountable for what they do? Is it possible that Christians today have unknowingly been inoculated with the notion of the hippy counterculture, which was generated as a reaction to the formal hypocritical pressures of society, that there is nothing evil of itself, that there are no standards, and that nothing is really holy, for there are no absolutes?

Could it be that the desire to curve the church into accepting woman as pastors has driven pastors to neuter the Bible and completely erase the lines of demarcation between the holy and the profane? Are the clergy losing their bearings? Listen: "Her priests have violated my law, and have profaned mine holy things: they have put no difference between the holy and profane, neither have they shewed *difference* between the unclean and the clean, and have hid their eyes from my sabbaths, and I am profaned among them" (Ezek. 22:26).

But irrespective of the warnings, admonitions, and severe consequences, there were always those like Jeroboam who determined that what God had ordained was of no consequence. So, using religion as a cloak, he blatantly debased the sacred in order to maintain his position in Israel. "Whereupon the king took counsel, and made two calves *of* gold, and said unto them, It is too much for you to go up to Jerusalem: behold thy gods, O Israel, which brought thee up out of the land of Egypt. And he set the one in Bethel, and the other put he in Dan. And this thing became a sin: for the people went *to worship* before the one, *even* unto Dan. And he made an house of high places, and made priests of the lowest of the people, which were not of the sons of Levi. And Jeroboam ordained a feast in the eighth month, on the fifteenth day of the month, like unto the feast that *is* in Judah, and he offered upon the altar. So did he in Bethel, sacrificing unto the calves that he had made: and he placed in Bethel the priests of the high places which he had made. So he offered upon the altar which he had made in Bethel the fifteenth day of the eighth month, *even* in the month which he had devised of his own heart; and ordained a feast unto the children of Israel: and he offered upon the altar, and burnt incense" (1 Kings 12:28–33).

Because God had not reproved him for his actions, he was emboldened in his rebellion. God oftentimes allowed apostasy to try the hearts of His people. Thus, the record states: "After this thing Jeroboam returned not from his evil way, but made again of the lowest of the people priests of the high places: whosoever would, he consecrated him, and he became *one* of the priests of the high places" (1 Kings 13:33). While God permitted Jeroboam to carry out his apostasy, it was a matter of time before he suffered God's retribution. "And this thing became sin unto the house of Jeroboam, even to cut *it* off, and to destroy *it* from off the face of the earth" (1 Kings 13:34).

> *Is it possible that the desire to bring God down to a common level to impress people with His kindness and goodness may rob Him of His rightful position as the Potentate of the universe, worthy of reverence and respect?*

This pluralistic tactic of the enemy continued to plague God's people and was in full vogue when Christ came. It was the common practice of the Jewish leaders to substitute human reasonings for God's commands. Jesus said: "Howbeit in vain do they worship me, teaching *for* doctrines the commandments of men. For laying aside the commandment of God, ye hold the traditions of men, *as* the washing of cups: and many other such like things ye do" (Mark 7:7, 8). The story of the rich man and Lazarus, in Luke 16, describes Lazarus's going to Abraham's bosom and the rich man's going to a place of torment, where he still had easy access to Abraham. This parable used a Greek concept of life after death that had been integrated by the leaders into the Jewish belief system. Changing what God claimed as holy and applying that holiness to something else became their *modus operandi*. To this, Jesus' condemnation was clear. "Woe unto you, *ye* blind guides, which say, Whosoever shall swear by the temple, it is nothing; but whosoever shall swear by the gold of the temple, he is a debtor! *Ye* fools and blind: for whether is greater, the gold, or the temple that sanctifieth the gold? And, Whosoever shall swear by the altar, it is nothing; but whosoever sweareth by the gift that is upon it, he is guilty. *Ye* fools and blind: for whether *is* greater, the gift, or the altar that sanctifieth the gift? Whoso therefore shall swear by the altar, sweareth by it, and by all things thereon. And whoso shall swear by the temple, sweareth by it, and by him that dwelleth therein. And he that shall swear by heaven, sweareth by the throne of God, and by him that sitteth thereon" (Matt. 23:16–22).

Though Christ worked at reversing or eliminating Satan's twists to the truth, the devil obviously found this strategy effective in neutralizing God's Word. Paul ardently fought against the Judaizer's attempts to remove God's truth by substituting for it the religious rites that had ended with Christ on the cross. He wrote: "And you, being dead in your sins and the uncircumcision of your flesh, hath he quickened together with him, having forgiven you all trespasses; blotting out the handwriting of ordinances that was against us, which was contrary to us, and took it out of the way, nailing it to his cross; *and* having spoiled principalities and powers, he made a shew of them openly, triumphing over them in it. Let no man therefore judge you in meat, or in drink, or in respect of an holyday, or of the new moon, or of the sabbath *days:* which are a shadow of things to come; but the body *is* of Christ. Let no man beguile you of your reward in a voluntary humility and worshipping of angels, intruding into those things which he hath not seen, vainly puffed up by his fleshly mind" (Col. 2:13–18). Paul warned the Galatians: "I marvel that ye are so soon removed from him that called you into the grace of Christ unto another gospel: Which is not another; but there be some that trouble you, and would pervert the gospel of Christ. But though we, or an angel from heaven, preach any other gospel unto you than that which we have preached unto you, let him be accursed. As we said before, so say I now again, If any *man* preach any other gospel unto you than that ye have received, let him be accursed" (Gal. 1:6–9).

This artful ploy of mixing truth with error, the holy and the profane, became Satan's chief method of fighting against Christ, apart from temptation itself. His greatest success was in leading insiders to twist the Scriptures. Peter charged, "Even as our beloved brother Paul also according to the wisdom given unto him hath written unto you; as also in all *his* epistles, speaking in them of these things; in which are some things hard to be understood, which they that are unlearned and unstable wrest, as *they do* also the other scriptures, unto their own destruction" (2 Peter 3:15, 16). Jesus commanded John the Revelator to reveal the inroads made by the devil on the church through apostates. He wrote: "But I have a few things against thee, because thou hast there them that hold the doctrine of Balaam, who taught Balac to cast a stumblingblock before the children of Israel, to eat things sacrificed unto idols, and to commit fornication. So hast thou also them that hold the doctrine of the Nicolaitans, which thing I hate. ... Notwithstanding I have a few things against thee, because thou sufferest that woman Jezebel, which calleth herself a prophetess, to teach and to seduce my servants to commit fornication, and to eat things sacrificed unto idols" (Rev. 2:14, 15, 20).

The final conflict between Christ and Satan will be fought within the confines of defining what is truth and what is error. "Come hither," the angel said, "I will shew unto thee the judgment of the great whore that sitteth upon many waters: With whom the kings of the earth have committed fornication, and the inhabitants of the earth have been made drunk with the wine of her fornication" (Rev. 17:1, 2). This child of the archenemy of souls will accomplish the seduction of the world by her mixture of truth and error. Through her, the archenemy will blend truth and error so thoroughly that the mixture's potent effect will succeed in the overthrow of those that do not adhere strictly to a "thus saith the Lord." In the final contest, the enemy, by his temptations, will have gained control of the majority of earth's population. Since he will not be able to gain control of the faithful through his temptations, he will resort to miracles and false and misleading teachings. Satan's church will win the world through its mixed wine. Blending truth and error—the holy and the profane—so closely that, unless they know the Scriptures very well and adhere to them, it will be possible for Satan to deceive even "the very elect" (Matt. 24:24).

The issue at hand is not really about women, but rather something much greater. This emotional issue is being used to cover up the underlining attack on God and His holy Word. By using women to take over men's role the enemy is actually making of none effect the order God established. It will, in its finality, cast doubt on the Bible as a reliable guide of truth. Once the Bible is held subject to question, the soul will lose its anchor, for, without the Word's validity, truth will become subjective. In declaring the Bible sexist, its Author is indited as well. Hence, its inspiration will be held suspect. Once the enemy succeeds in reaching that threshold, the world will be taken in by his delusion. A god of man's own making will replace the true God. But those that hold to the Scriptures as completely inspired will find a sure foundation to stand on. In a world where nothing is trustworthy, the Bible-believing soul will find safety and certainty that will take him through the final events of earth's history. In a "thus saith the Lord," they will insure their salvation. "As we learn more and more of what God is, and of what we ourselves are in His sight, we shall fear and tremble before Him. Let men of today take warning from the fate of those who in ancient times presumed to make free with that which God had declared sacred. When the Israelites ventured to open the ark on its return from the land of the Philistines, their irreverent daring was signally punished."[54] "The whole Bible is a revelation of the glory of God in Christ. Received, believed, obeyed, it is the great instrumentality in the transformation of character. It is the grand stimulus, the constraining force, that quickens the physical, mental, and spiritual powers, and directs the life into right channels."[55]

The very essence of the three angels of Revelation chapter 14 is salvation by distinction. Restore the God of the Scriptures to His rightful position with His combined love and justice, and His mercy and power will accomplish for the trembling soul all that it needs. Dilute His attributes to meet man where he is, rather than bringing man up to where God is, and

---

54 E. G. White, *The Ministry of Healing,* pp. 435, 436.
55 E. G. White, *The Ministry of Healing,* pp. 435, 436.

you set him up to an unholy corruptible nature that is unable to save itself. Yes, "fear God, and give glory to him" (Rev. 14:7).

"The Lord would have his people trust in him and abide in his love, but that does not mean that we shall have no fear or misgivings. Some seem to think that if a man has a wholesome fear of the judgments of God, it is a proof that he is destitute of faith; but this is not so. A proper fear of God, in believing his threatenings, works the peaceable fruits of righteousness, by causing the trembling soul to flee to Jesus. Many ought to have this

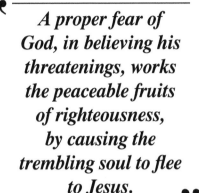

A proper fear of God, in believing his threatenings, works the peaceable fruits of righteousness, by causing the trembling soul to flee to Jesus.

spirit today, and turn to the Lord with humble contrition, for the Lord has not given so many terrible threatenings, pronounced so severe judgments in his word, simply to have them recorded, but he means what he says. One says, 'Horror hath taken hold upon me because of the wicked that forsake thy law.' [Ps. 119:53.] Paul says, 'Knowing therefore the terror of the Lord, we persuade men.' [2 Cor. 5:11.]"[56]

---

56 E. G. White, *Review and Herald*, Oct. 21, 1890.

10.

Men as Ordained Pastors or Ministers

T he Bible reveals that, in the Old Testament, only men were priests, or elders, which were, at times, referred to as pastors (Jer. 2:8; 3:15). Likewise, in the New Testament, only men were apostles, elders, ministers, or pastors (Eph. 4:11; 1 Peter 2:25; 1 Tim. 3:1, 2; Titus 1:7). There was no exception—even in the dispersion of Judah by Babylon in the days of Jeremiah. The Lord inspired him to write, "Neither shall the priests the Levites want a man before me to offer burnt offerings, and to kindle meat offerings, and to do sacrifice continually" (Jer. 33:18). Only the sons of Aaron could eat of the sin and trespass offerings. "All the males among the children of Aaron shall eat of it. *It shall be* a statute for ever in your generations concerning the offerings of the LORD made by fire: every one that toucheth them shall be holy. ... All the males among the priests shall eat thereof: it *is* most holy" (Lev. 6:18, 29). The gender specific language makes crystal clear God's design concerning these offerings.

The word "minister" and "ministry" are not always synonymous. The first time the word *minister* appears in the Bible is in Exodus 24:13, which reads, "And Moses rose up, and his minister Joshua: and Moses went up into the mount of God." The Hebrew word is *"shârath"* (Strong's #8334), pronounced, *shaw-rath*. In this instance, the Hebrew word, as found in Strong's Hebrew and Chaldee Dictionary, can mean, "minister (v) 62, minister (n) 17, serve 8, servant 5, service 3." In the same concordance, the Hebrew word used in Exodus 28:1 is *kâhan* (Strong's #3547), which is pronounced *kaw-han*. It means "to act as a priest, or minister in a priest's office." Here is the verse: "And take thou unto thee Aaron thy brother, and his sons with him, from among the children of Israel, that he may minister unto me in the priest's office, *even* Aaron, Nadab and Abihu, Eleazar and Ithamar, Aaron's sons." In Exodus 24:13 and 28:1, two different words are translated into the same word in English.

However, in the original language, one word signified a person who served, while the other word had to do with carrying out the office of a priest. In the King James Version, the English word "minister" is found 99 times in 97 verses in the Old and New Testaments. All except for two of these (Eph. 4:29; 1 Tim. 1:4, which use the word to mean "contributing") have to do with the male gender either being a minister or doing ministry.

Not only is the male gender ordained by God to serve as the spiritual leader in the Old Testament, but it is also a practice ordained in the New Testament. Paul's inspired counsel validates this. In writing to Timothy, he speaks of the matter of gender when addressing the issue of who is qualified to be a bishop. After writing about the expected manner in which godly women should carry themselves, he elaborates on the spiritual relationship and role of women in connection with men. "But I suffer not a woman to teach, nor to usurp authority over the man, but to be in silence. For Adam was first formed, then Eve. And Adam was not deceived, but the woman being deceived was in the transgression. Notwithstanding she shall be saved in childbearing, [in fulfillment of the promise of Genesis 3:15], if they continue in faith and charity and holiness with sobriety" (1 Tim. 2:12–15).

> **Not only is the male gender ordained by God to serve as the spiritual leader in the Old Testament, but it is also a practice ordained in the New Testament.**

Today, those who choose to dismiss God's recorded orders have varying motives for doing so. Perhaps the most alarming is the one that has an air of spirituality and avoids indictment by stating, "The Lord did not say that it could not be done, so it must be okay." If questionable permissible acts come by way of God "not saying that it could not be done," then the sky's the limit, and all are right in their own eyes. This attitude is mentioned as a deplorable condition in the Bible. For example, "The man Micah had an house of gods, and made an ephod, and teraphim, and consecrated one of his sons, who became his priest. In those days *there was* no king in Israel, *but* every man did *that which was* right in his own eyes" (Judges 17:5, 6). It is important to note that this prevailing condition of religious disorder, in particular, marks a departure from what God had established by setting up gods and unsanctified priests. The same was true as pertaining to civil disorder in the absence of leadership. "In those days *there was* no king in Israel: every man did *that which was* right in his own eyes" (Judges 21:25). In the absence of civil leadership, doing what is right in one's own eyes brings anarchy and disorder. In the presence of spiritual leadership, such religious disorder is outright rebellion or heresy and apostasy. Both conditions point to none other than the master archenemy.

11.

Old Testament Transition to the New Testament

When Christ died on the cross, the curtain of the temple was torn in half from top to bottom (Matt. 27:50, 51). This opened the way for the New Testament church to replace the Old Testament system of worship (Acts 7:38). "Behold, the days come, saith the LORD, that I will make a new covenant with the house of Israel, and with the house of Judah: Not according to the covenant that I made with their fathers in the day *that* I took them by the hand to bring them out of the land of Egypt; which my covenant they brake, although I was an husband unto them, saith the LORD: But this *shall be* the covenant that I will make with the house of Israel; After those days, saith the LORD, I will put my law in their inward parts, and write it in their hearts; and will be their God, and they shall be my people" (Jer. 31:31–33). Paul confirmed this transition when he wrote to Hebrew believers in Christ: "This *is* the covenant that I will make with them after those days, saith the Lord, I will put my laws into their hearts, and in their minds will I write them; … Having therefore, brethren, boldness to enter into the holiest by the blood of Jesus, by a new and living way, which he hath consecrated for us, through the veil, that is to say, his flesh; and *having* an high priest over the house of God" (Heb. 10:16, 19–21).

Inasmuch as the Old Testament church came to an end with the death of Christ, the ordinances would also cease. "If those ordinances depart from before me, saith the LORD, *then* the seed of Israel also shall cease from being a nation before me for ever" (Jer. 31:36). That is why Paul wrote to the Colossians: "Blotting out the handwriting of ordinances that was against us, which was contrary to us, and took it out of the way, nailing it to his cross; and having spoiled principalities and powers, he made a shew of them openly, triumphing over them in it. Let no man therefore judge you in meat, or in drink, or in respect of an holyday, or of the new moon, or of the sabbath *days*: which are a shadow of things to come; but the body is of

Christ" (Col. 2:14–17). The ordinances that were "against us" were written in the "book of the law." We find this description in Deuteronomy 31:26, where God said, "Take this book of the law, and put it in the side of the ark of the covenant of the LORD your God, that it may be there for a witness against thee." Notice that it was the book of the law that contained the ordinances that was "against thee." It was in this "book" that all the ceremonial laws, the curses, and sacrifices were recorded (Deut. 28:58, 61; 29:20, 21; 30:10). This "book" is called the Torah, Pentateuch, or the five books of Moses, which are "the first five books of the Hebrew Bible, named: Genesis, Exodus, Leviticus, Numbers and Deuteronomy."[57] It was the ceremonies, written in the "book of the law," that would be cut off when the Messiah would be "be cut off, but not for himself" (Dan. 9:26). As verse 27 says, "He shall confirm the covenant with many for one week: and in the midst of the week he shall cause the sacrifice and the oblation to cease."

These ordinances were typologies of Christ, which met their fulfillment and ended in Christ. Let me show you a comparison of the type and the antitype, the symbol and the fulfillment, below:

Lamb	Gen. 22:8; Exod. 12:3	Lamb of God	John 1:29
Passover	Exod. 12:11	Christ our Passover	1 Cor. 5:7
Firstfruits	Lev. 23:10, 17, 20	Christ the First Fruit	1 Cor. 15:20–23; Eph. 4:8
Feast of Tabernacles, dwell among them	Exod. 25:8	Dwelt among us	John 1:14
The Veil	Exod. 26:31	His Flesh	Heb. 10:20
Unleavened Bread	Exod. 34:18	Bread of Life	John 6:35
Light	Exod. 13:21; Exod. 25:37	I am the Light of the World	John 8:12
Priest	Gen. 14:18; Lev. 15:30	Jesus the Priest	Heb. 7:21; 8:1; 10:21

---

57 "What are the sections of the New Testament?" https://1ref.us/1v0, accessed 12/9/21; "Torah," at https://1ref.us/1v1, accessed 12/9/2021.

There were several practices or laws that were not swallowed up by Christ's sacrifice. These were the Decalogue, or the Ten Commandments, which are God's eternal standard of righteousness. Regarding this standard, Paul wrote, "Do we then make void the law through faith? God forbid: yea, we establish the law" (Rom. 3:31. He also wrote: "Owe no man any thing, but to love one another: for he that loveth another hath fulfilled the law. For this, Thou shalt not commit adultery, Thou shalt not kill, Thou shalt not steal, Thou shalt not bear false witness, Thou shalt not covet; and if *there be* any other commandment, it is briefly comprehended in this saying, namely, Thou shalt love thy neighbour as thyself. Love worketh no ill to his neighbour: therefore love *is* the fulfilling of the law" (Rom. 13:8–10). The health laws likewise transcended the change, as is evidenced in Paul's words, "Know ye not that ye are the temple of God, and *that* the Spirit of God dwelleth in you? If any man defile the temple of God, him shall God destroy; for the temple of God is holy, which *temple* ye are" (1 Cor. 3:16, 17). In this regard, there are several verses that have often been misused. Peter's refusal to eat anything "common or unclean" in Acts 10:14 makes it clear that, in his entire life— including his three and a half years as a disciple of Christ— he always followed the biblical admonition to abstain from unclean animals as food. In verses 28, he clarified what the vision meant when he said: "And he said unto them, Ye know how that it is an unlawful thing for a man that is a Jew to keep company, or come unto one of another nation; but God hath shewed me that I should not call any man common or unclean." Paul's statement to Timothy, in 1 Timothy 4:1–4, is also misunderstood. There Paul is arguing for the preservation of marriage as well as clarifying that those who are influenced by seducing spirits recommend abandoning both marriage (Gen. 2:23–25) and the "meats" (Greek *brōma*, meaning "foods") created by God to be received with thanksgiving (see Gen. 1:29; 3:18; 7:2; 9:3). It is these foods that, he says, are "sanctified by the word of God and prayer."

The earthly priesthood of the house of Aaron, in the Old Testament, met its fulfillment and end in Christ, but the need for the ministry and the function of the ministry did not. In the old dispensation, God chose men to serve in ministry. In those days, they were called priests (Jer. 2:8), elders (Num. 11:25), or shepherds and pastors (Jer. 23:1). Regarding this fact, Paul wrote: "Then verily the first *covenant* had also ordinances of divine service, and a worldly sanctuary. For there was a tabernacle made; the first, wherein *was* the candlestick, and the table, and the shewbread;

which is called the sanctuary. And after the second veil, the tabernacle which is called the Holiest of all; which had the golden censer, and the ark of the covenant overlaid round about with gold, wherein *was* the golden pot that had manna, and Aaron's rod that budded, and the tables of the covenant; And over it the cherubims of glory shadowing the mercyseat; of which we cannot now speak particularly. Now when these things were thus ordained, the priests went always into the first tabernacle, accomplishing the service *of God*. But into the second *went* the high priest alone once every year, not without blood, which he offered for himself, and *for* the errors of the people: The Holy Ghost this signifying, that the way into the holiest of all was not yet made manifest, while as the first tabernacle was yet standing: which *was* a figure for the time then present, in which were offered both gifts and sacrifices, that could not make him that did the service perfect, as pertaining to the conscience; *which stood* only in meats and drinks, and divers washings, and carnal ordinances, imposed *on them* until the time of reformation" (Heb. 9:1–10). This time of reformation did come. "But Christ being come an high priest of good things to come, by a greater and more perfect tabernacle, not made with hands, that is to say, not of this building; neither by the blood of goats and calves, but by his own blood he entered in once into the holy place, having obtained eternal redemption *for us*" (Heb. 9:11, 12). No wonder Paul was inspired to clarify to the Hebrew believers an understanding that would pave the way for the new dispensation.

There was no lapse of time for the apostles in implementing changes. They immediately began the process in replacing Judas, the fallen apostle (see Acts 1:13–25). Then, when Paul plunged into the work of spreading the gospel, the "right hands" (Gal. 2:9) were extended to him to continue to extend the new order among the newly converted Gentiles. Their understanding of this transition from priests to apostles is evidenced by their extending the hand of authority. Luke reported, "And when they had ordained them elders in every church, and had prayed with fasting, they commended them to the Lord, on whom they believed" (Acts 14:23). Paul also encouraged Timothy: "Let the elders that rule well be counted worthy of double honour, especially they who labour in the word and doctrine" (1 Tim. 5:17). This divinely ordained New Testament practice filled the vacuum created by the vacating of the priesthood, thus making room for the new dispensation. Christ then became the heavenly priest, making it essential to ordain a New Testament ministry. As He met with His followers prior to His death, He chose twelve men to serve the new church in ministry. For good reason, Luke's account says, "He sat down, and the twelve apostles with him" (Luke 22:14). He then said to them, "And I appoint unto you a kingdom, as my Father hath appointed unto me; that ye may eat and drink at my table in my kingdom, and sit on thrones judging the twelve tribes of Israel" (Luke 22:29, 30). These twelve men were appointed by Christ by ordination to continue the work of the priesthood as apostles or elders to serve His flock.

Even at the ascension of Christ into heaven, the angel's address was to men. The record states: "Until the day in which he was taken up, after that he through the Holy Ghost had given commandments unto the apostles whom he had chosen: To whom also he shewed himself alive after his passion by many infallible proofs, being seen of them forty days, and speaking of the things pertaining to the kingdom of God: And, being assembled together with *them*, commanded them that they should not depart from Jerusalem, but wait for the promise of the Father, which, *saith he*, ye have heard of me. For John truly baptized with water; but ye shall be baptized with the Holy Ghost not many days hence. ... And when he had spoken these things, while they beheld, he was taken up; and a cloud received him out of their sight. And while they looked stedfastly toward heaven as he went up, behold, two men stood by them in white apparel; Which also said, Ye men of Galilee, why stand ye gazing up into heaven? This same Jesus, which is taken up from you into heaven, shall so come in like manner as ye have seen him go into heaven" (Acts 1:2–4, 9–11).

The support of the ministry was another practice that did not become obsolete for it was not among the shadows of the sacrificial services. In this regard, Paul addresses the financial support of those who would be selected to serve in the gospel ministry of the New Testament. He wrote, "Do ye not know that they which minister about holy things live *of the things* of the temple? And they which wait at the altar are partakers with the altar? Even so hath the Lord ordained that they which preach the gospel should live of the gospel" (1 Cor. 9:13, 14). Obviously, Paul is referring to the Old Testament God-ordained means of financial support for the Old Covenant priesthood. Moses wrote: "And, behold, I have given the children of Levi all the tenth in Israel for an inheritance, for their service which they serve, *even* the service of the tabernacle of the congregation. ... Thus speak unto the Levites, and say unto them, When ye take of the children of Israel the tithes which I have given you from them for your inheritance, then ye shall offer up an heave offering of it for the LORD, even a tenth part of the tithe" (Num. 18:21, 26; see also Lev. 27:30, 32; 2 Chron. 31:4–10; Mal. 3:10, 11; Heb. 7:5). Quoting Deuteronomy 25:4, Paul wrote, "Thou shalt not muzzle the ox that treadeth out the corn. And, The labourer *is* worthy of his reward" (1 Tim. 5:18). Jesus also endorsed this practice when He said, "for ye pay tithe of mint and anise and cummin, and have omitted the weightier *matters* of the law, judgment, mercy, and faith: these ought ye to have done, and not to leave the other undone" (Matt. 23:23). To the disciples He said, "And in the same house remain, eating and drinking such things as they give: for the labourer is worthy of his hire. Go not from house to house" (Luke 10:7).

The observance of the Passover was transitioned into what is called "the Lord's Supper," or "the Last Supper." Inasmuch as Jesus was the Lamb that was sacrificed, there would no longer be any need to sacrifice animals. Instead, Christ transitioned this rite into the eating of bread and the drinking of the "new wine," called grape juice today. And rather than celebrating the Passover on Nisan 14, Paul was instructed to write, "For I have received of the Lord that which also I delivered unto you, That the Lord Jesus the *same* night in which he was betrayed took bread: And when he had given thanks, he brake *it*, and said, Take, eat: this is my body, which is broken for you: this do in remembrance of me. After the same manner also *he took* the cup, when he had supped, saying, This cup is the new testament in my blood: this do ye, as oft as ye drink *it*, in remembrance of me. For as often as ye eat this bread, and drink this cup, ye do shew the Lord's death till he come" (1 Cor. 11:23–26).

Christ, the Creator and Redeemer and Head of His church, laid down for His followers by precept and example the essentials of the faith. To alter or change any of those essentials of His ordained order is to supplant and undercut His intended purposes by removing or maintaining what He considered crucial to His church and its followers. Through His death, resurrection, ascension, and enthronement on the right hand of the Majesty in heaven, Jesus, the One to whom the earthly priesthood pointed (see Heb. 8:1–5; 9:6–11), continued the priesthood as the genuine priest in heaven. Paul therefore wrote: "If therefore perfection were by the Levitical priesthood, (for under it the people received the law,) what further need *was there* that another priest should rise after the order of Melchisedec, and not be called after the order of Aaron? For the priesthood being changed, there is made of necessity a change also of the law. For he of whom these things are spoken pertaineth to another tribe, of which no man gave attendance at the altar. For *it is* evident that our Lord sprang out of Juda; of which tribe Moses spake nothing concerning priesthood. And it is yet far more evident: for that after the similitude of Melchisedec there ariseth another priest, Who is made, not after the law of a carnal commandment, but after the power of an endless life. For he testifieth, Thou *art* a priest for ever after the order of Melchisedec. For there is verily a disannulling of the commandment going before for the weakness and unprofitableness thereof. For the law made nothing perfect, but the bringing in of a better hope *did;* by the which we draw nigh unto God. And inasmuch as not without an oath *he was made priest:* (for those priests were made without an oath; but this with an oath by him that said unto him, The Lord sware and will not repent, Thou *art* a priest for ever after the order of Melchisedec:) By so much was Jesus made a surety of a better testament. And they truly were many priests, because they were not suffered to continue by reason of death: But this *man*, because he continueth ever, hath an unchangeable priesthood" (Heb. 7:11–24). "But now hath he obtained a more excellent ministry, by how much also he is the mediator of a better covenant, which was established upon better promises" (Heb. 8:6).

In the Old Testament, God pronounced over His people: "And ye shall be unto me a kingdom of priests, and an holy nation" (Exod. 19:6). In the New Testament, God pronounced the same standing for the Christian Church. He did this by conveying the same blessing in the New Testament: "But ye *are* a chosen generation, a royal priesthood, an holy nation, a peculiar people; that ye should shew forth the praises of him who hath called you out of darkness into his marvellous light: Which in time past *were* not a people, but *are* now the people of God: which had not obtained mercy, but now have obtained mercy" (1 Peter 2:9, 10). There was no question in the minds of the apostles that Jewish Israel was replaced by the multi-national Israel. Paul wrote, "For in Christ Jesus neither circumcision availeth any thing, nor uncircumcision, but a new creature. And as many as walk according to this rule, peace *be* on them, and mercy, and upon the Israel of God" (Gal. 6:15, 16). And to the Ephesians he wrote, "According as he hath chosen us in him before the foundation of the world, that we should be holy and without blame before him in love: Having predestinated us unto the adoption of children by Jesus Christ to himself, according to the good pleasure of his will" (Eph. 1:4, 5). "That the Gentiles should be fellowheirs, and of the same body, and partakers of his promise in Christ by the gospel: Whereof I was made a minister, according to the gift of the grace of God given unto me by the effectual working of his power" (Eph. 3:6, 7).

This transition Paul clarifies by certifying who was a true Israelite or Jew. To the Romans he wrote: "For he is not a Jew, which is one outwardly; neither *is that* circumcision, which is outward in the flesh: But he *is* a Jew, which is one inwardly; and circumcision *is that* of the heart, in the spirit, *and* not in the letter; whose praise *is* not of men, but of God" (Rom. 2:28, 29). Then, continuing the same theme, he wrote, "For they *are* not all Israel, which are of Israel: Neither, because they are the seed of Abraham, *are they* all children: but, In Isaac shall thy seed be called. That is, They which are the children of the flesh, these *are* not the children of God: but the children of the promise are counted for the seed" (Rom. 9:6–8).

And just as in the Old Testament, only those who were chosen served in the kingdom of the nation led by priests, the same is true in the New Testament. God would lead a holy church not by earthly kings but by Christ as our High Priest and with ordained men chosen and set apart to serve God's church. In Peter's inspired declaration, Christ conferred upon the New Testament believers the same standing with God that the Old Testament church had—with the same conditions of faithfulness and obedience. That is why Paul wrote to the Philippians, "For we are the circumcision, which worship God in the spirit, and rejoice in Christ Jesus, and have no confidence in the flesh" (Phil. 3:3). This was, of course, a confirmation of the prophecy involuntarily declared by the high priest in that fateful meeting when seeking to get rid of Jesus. "Caiaphas, being the high priest that same year, said unto them, Ye know nothing at all, nor consider that it is expedient for us, that one man should die for the people, and that the whole nation perish not. And this spake he not of himself: but being high priest that year, he prophesied that Jesus should die for that nation; And not for that nation only, but that also he should gather together in one the children of God that were scattered abroad" (John 11:49–52).

Of deep significance is the revelation that the leader of the New Testament church was not Peter, but James the brother of Jesus. Why

James? I suggest that it had to do with the Jewish practice of the succession of the priesthood. It had to come through the family line. James was a brother of Jesus. "Is not this the carpenter's son? is not his mother called Mary? and his brethren, James, and Joses, and Simon, and Judas? And his sisters, are they not all with us? Whence then hath this *man* all these things" (Matt. 13:55, 56)? Paul wrote, "But other of the apostles saw I none, save James the Lord's brother" (Gal. 1:19). This James was not James who was the brother of John, for Herod had "killed James the brother of John with the sword" (Acts 12:1, 2).

Peter recognized James as the leader of the church. This was made evident in the incident of his imprisonment. After an angel had miraculously delivered Peter out of prison, he made his way to where the believers were gathered together praying for him. "Peter knocked at the door of the gate, a damsel came to hearken, named Rhoda" (Acts 12:13). When she opened the door, he said to her, "Go shew these things unto James, and to the brethren. And he departed, and went into another place" (Acts 12:17). Why did he specifically name James? Because he was the recognized leader.

There was potential of a schism in the early church due to theological questions. To meet the emergency, the apostles met with Paul and others who had attended the meeting in Jerusalem with him. After each had presented their particular side of the issue, James gave his judgment on the matter. "James answered, saying, Men *and* brethren, hearken unto me: Simeon hath declared how God at the first did visit the Gentiles, to take out of them a people for his name. ... Wherefore my sentence is, that we trouble not them, which from among the Gentiles are turned to God" (Acts 15:13, 14, 19). As the presiding leader, he delivered his sentence, and "then pleased it the apostles and elders, with the whole church" (Acts 15:22). Later on, Luke wrote about their travels and return to Jerusalem: "There went with us also *certain* of the disciples of Caesarea, and brought with them one Mnason of Cyprus, an old disciple, with whom we should lodge. And when we were come to Jerusalem, the brethren received us gladly. And the *day* following Paul went in with us unto James; and all the elders were present" (Acts 21:16–18). Paul later stated, "And when James, Cephas [Peter], and John, who seemed to be pillars, perceived the grace that was given unto me, they gave to me and Barnabas the right hands of fellowship" (Gal. 2:9).

> *New Testament believers viewed themselves as the fulfillment of the new order predicted in the Word and as the continuance of the true Jewish faith.*

This ecclesiastical benediction on the New Testament church was confirmed by James' sentence: "Men *and* brethren hearken unto me: Simeon hath declared how God at the first did visit the Gentiles, to take out of them a people for his name. And to this agree the words of the prophets; as it is written, after this I will return, and will build again the tabernacle of David, which is fallen down; and I will build again the ruins thereof, and I will set it up: That the residue of men might seek after the Lord, and all the Gentiles, upon whom my name is called, saith the Lord, who doeth all these things. Known unto God are all his works from the beginning of the world" (Acts 15:13–18). Based on the foregoing evidence, it is crystal clear that the New Testament believers viewed themselves as the fulfillment of the new order predicted in the Word and as the continuance of the true Jewish faith. They also recognized the transition from the Old Testament ecclesiastical order to the New Testament Apostolic system of leadership in God's church with ecclesiastical authority over doctrines and church order.

12.

Biblical Headship

The headship of the home has become a recent debate, and it is being challenged among the ranks of Christianity. The lack of appropriate male leadership may have contributed to the problem. However, while there are those who are now questioning the headship of the family and of the church, they need to consider this: the Ten Commandments, which carry with them the consequences of life or death (see Deut. 11:27, 28), are God's directives given primarily to men. It is the men who are considered by God to be the heads of families. The second commandment addresses the "iniquity of the fathers upon the children unto the third and fourth generation" (Exod. 20:5). Notice it makes no mention of the mothers. The prevalence of iniquity is placed solely on the shoulders of the fathers.

The fourth commandment also addresses the head of the home. The Sabbath and marriage are the only two institutions that are still with us from the Creation. Christ ordained both! (See Gen. 2:1–4, 24–25; Col. 1:13–17.) And while women are included under the term "thou," men are the main object of the directive. This conclusion comes from the mention of the phrase, "nor thy son, nor thy daughter." The counsel from God concerning "sons and daughters" was directed to the fathers. He held them responsible for their children. Of the ninety-four times the phrase "sons and daughters" is mentioned in the Bible, all but two are relating to being born to the man or the father. The omission or exclusion of the mother or of women in the fourth commandment echoes the second commandment's placing of responsibility primarily on the fathers. And while the women are all inclusive in the directives, it is by virtue of a second position rather than the primary role. Since women are considered to be under man's guardianship (Gen. 3:16), the fourth commandment includes them.

The tenth commandment is also male directed. "Thou shalt not covet thy neighbor's wife … nor any thing that *is* thy neighbor's" (Exod. 20:17). This is not to suggest that women or wives are free from this restriction, seeing that it was Eve's coveting of the forbidden fruit and its supposed magical power that brought the downfall of Adam and, consequently, of the human race. Here again the weight of constraint is placed on the husband. The women's curb in this matter therefore is implied due to the husbands honoring this God-given admonition. In this commandment, "anything that is thy neighbor's" includes the wife. She is considered as belonging to him.

Even when it comes to the parent's honor, the father again is first mentioned and then the mother. Here, in the fifth commandment, Christ enjoins upon the children to honor the family unit and its order. *Do away with the headship, and you will have to re-write the commandments.* In the King James Version of the Bible, the word "fathers" appears 546 times in 514 verses, while the singular form of the word, "father," appears 979 times in 856 verses. The word "mother," on the other hand, appears a total of 245 times in 216 verses, while the plural form, "mothers," appears only eight times in seven verses. The sheer numbers of mentions of fathers over mothers suggests that inspiration leans heavily on the role of the father in his designated role as head of the families.

God established marriage, and the perpetuity of the marital relationship was to continue with the man leaving his father and mother and cleaving unto his wife (Gen. 2:24, 25). Every subsequent biblically recognized marriage from that of Adam and Eve down through the ages maintained the same order of the male leading out in the arrangement God has established. This is an order that Christ himself acknowledged and confirmed four thousand years after the inception of marriage (see Matt. 19:4–6), and it is still being followed by the majority of the cultures of the world.

The origin of skills, such as making and living in tents, and the occupation of cattlemen are traced back to fathers (Gen. 4:20). Making musical instruments is also credited to the fathers and not to mothers (verse 21). The same is true of the origin of nations (Gen. 9:18; 17:4, 5). Though Sarah would be the one giving birth to Isaac, it was the man Abraham who was declared to be the father of nations (Gen. 17:4, 5). When people died, it was their father's resting place that was designated as their resting place (Gen. 15:15; 47:30; 49:29; 2 Chron. 21:1). Even the land of people's origin was apportioned as being the land of the fathers (Gen. 48:21). The same is true when it came to the designation of the heads of the tribes of Israel (see Exod. 6:14–25; 1 Chron. 4:38). In the New Testament, it was the fathers who were held responsible for crucifying the Lord (Acts 2:23, 36; 5:30). And it is the fathers who are admonished to be role models for the family and the flock (Eph. 6:4; Col. 3:21; 1 John 2:13, 14). The lordship of man included the ownership of land (Gen. 31:3).

Whenever God visited with His servants or His people, as a point of reference, He identified Himself as the same One who had a past relationship with the fathers (see Gen. 26:24; Exod. 3:6, 13–16; Matt. 22:32; Acts 7:32). The Promised Land likewise was promised to the fathers. "And it shall be when the LORD shall bring thee into the land of the Canaanites, and the Hittites, and the Amorites, and the Hivites, and the Jebusites, which he sware unto thy fathers to give thee, a land flowing with milk and honey, that thou shalt keep this service in this month. And it shall be when the LORD shall bring thee into the land of the Canaanites, as he sware unto thee and to thy fathers, and shall give it thee" (Exod. 13:5, 11; see also Deut. 4:37; 6:3, 10, 18; 12:1; and 19:18 for examples). In particular was the designation of the heads of houses. "And thou shalt write Aaron's name upon the rod of Levi: for one rod *shall be* for the head of the house of their fathers" (Num. 17:3).

While God held the men as the primary stewards of possessions of houses and lands (Lev. 25:41), they also bore the brunt of the responsibility for the sins of the family and of the nation (see Exod. 34:7; Lev. 26:39). "The LORD hath accomplished his fury; he hath poured out his fierce anger, and hath kindled a fire in Zion, and it hath devoured the foundations thereof. ... For the sins of her prophets, *and* the iniquities of her priests, that have shed the blood of the just in the midst of her, they have wandered *as* blind *men* in the streets, they have polluted themselves with blood, so that men could not touch their garments" (Lam. 4:11, 13, 14). The standing of the family with God was determined by the faithfulness or unfaithfulness of the father. "Then I will set my face against that man, and against his family, and will cut him off, and all that go a whoring after him, to commit whoredom with Molech, from among their people" (Lev. 20:5). To Ezekiel God said, "Son of man, I send thee to the children of Israel, to a rebellious nation that hath rebelled against me: they and their fathers have transgressed against me, *even* unto this very day" (Ezek. 2:3).

It is noteworthy that a woman who became an heiress to her father's possessions (should she be the only child) was required to marry a man of the same tribe in order to keep the said possessions within that particular tribe of her father. "And every daughter, that possesseth an inheritance in any tribe of the children of Israel, shall be wife unto one of the family of the tribe of her father, that the children of Israel may enjoy every man the inheritance of his fathers" (Num. 36:8).

Throughout the entirety of the Scriptures, God condescended to meet and talk with man (Num. 12:8) and to enter into agreements with him. In doing so, He sought to impress mankind with His willingness to treat man on an equal level with Himself. Hence, He entered into a mutual agreement with man called a covenant. The first covenant made by God was with Noah, who was the father and head of his family (Gen. 6:8; 9:9–17). Later, He established a covenant with Abraham (Gen. 15:18). God's reason for entering a covenant with Abraham was: "For I know him, that he will command his children and his household after him, and they shall keep the way of the LORD, to do justice and judgment; that the LORD may bring upon Abraham that which he hath spoken of him" (Gen. 18:19). A covenant was later on made with the elders or fathers, which were representatives of Israel as a nation (see Exod. 19:5–7; Heb. 8:8, 9). Moses admonished the men of Israel and said, "Keep therefore the words of this covenant, and do them, that ye may prosper in all that ye do. Ye stand this day all of you before the LORD your God; your captains of your tribes, your elders, and your officers, *with* all the men of Israel, Your little ones, your wives, and thy stranger that *is* in thy camp, from the hewer of thy wood unto the drawer of thy water: That thou shouldest enter into covenant with the LORD thy God, and into his oath, which the LORD thy God maketh with thee this day: That he may establish thee today for a people unto himself, and *that* he may be unto thee a God, as he hath said unto thee, and as he hath sworn unto thy fathers, to Abraham, to Isaac, and to Jacob. Neither with you only do I make this covenant and this oath; But with *him* that standeth here with us this day before the LORD our God, and also with *him* that *is* not here with us this day" (Deut. 29:9–15). The men were held responsible for ensuring that the families were adherents to the agreement made between God and His people, and they were chided when they failed to lead their families. "I will even punish that man and his house" (Jer. 23:34). This God-given responsibility even carried over to the disallowing a vow made by either the wife or the daughter (Num. 30:1–14). Ultimately, God held the men responsible for the outcome of such commitments (verse 15).

The heads of the military were also to be males. "Take ye the sum of all the congregation of the children of Israel, after their families, by the house of their fathers, with the number of *their* names, every male by their polls; From twenty years old and upward, all that are able to go forth to war in Israel: thou and Aaron shall number them by their armies. And with you there shall be a man of every tribe; every one head of the house of his fathers" (Num. 1:2–4). This order included the priesthood also (Exod. 6:25). Never was a woman in the Scriptures given the place or put in charge of the family unless it was caused by the death of the father or when the father was absent due to temporary travel.

Even after decades of the destruction of Israel as a nation and in spite of the influences of heathenistic cultures, the headship among the Jews was kept intact. Nehemiah's recognition and encouragement to the headship certifies its unchanging structure. He said, "And I looked, and rose up, and said unto the nobles, and to the rulers, and to the rest of the people, Be not ye afraid of them: remember the Lord, *which is* great and terrible, and fight for your brethren, your sons, and your daughters, your wives, and your houses" (Neh. 4:14).

Devout men and women in the New Testament acknowledged this established family headship. Mary, the honored vessel chosen to give birth to Earth's Redeemer, acknowledged and gladly submitted to the recognized order (see Luke 1:55, 69). Zacharias the priest, the father of John the Baptist, gave evidence of his understanding relative to the role of the father. He said: "Blessed *be* the Lord God of Israel; for He hath visited and redeemed His people, and hath raised up an horn of salvation for us in the house of his servant David; as he spake by the mouth of his holy prophets, which have been since the world began: that we should be saved from our enemies, and from the hand of all that hate us; to perform the mercy *promised* to our fathers, and to remember his holy covenant; the oath which He sware to our father Abraham" (Luke 1:68–73). Even the Samaritan woman, speaking to Christ at the well, pointed to the blessings that came to the Samaritans through the fathers (see John 4:20).

This God-ordained order continued to be recognized by Peter and John. In giving credit to the source of the lame man's healing Peter declared: "The God of Abraham, and of Isaac, and of Jacob, the God of our fathers ... For Moses truly said unto the fathers, A prophet shall the Lord your God raise up unto you of your brethren, like unto me; him shall ye hear in all things whatsoever he shall say unto you. ... Ye are the children of the prophets, and of the covenant which God made with our fathers" (Acts 3:13, 22, 25). "And he said, Men, brethren, and fathers, hearken; The God of glory appeared unto our father Abraham, when he was in Mesopotamia, before he dwelt in Charran" (Acts 7:2).

Since God is the One who established the headship of men in the family, tribe, and nation, wouldn't it seem more than reasonable to submit to that which He ordained? To reject the headship is to reject God who established the order of the family and of the nation. Hence Paul was inspired to write: "But I would have you know, that the head of every man is Christ; and the head of the woman *is* the man; and the head of Christ *is* God" (1 Cor. 11:3).

Headship in the Passover

❝ *Since God is the One who established the headship of men in the family, tribe, and nation, wouldn't it seem more than reasonable to submit to that which He ordained?* ❞

When the Israelites were ordered to prepare to leave Egypt, they were first instructed to celebrate the first Passover. God's instruction to Moses was: "Speak ye unto all the congregation of Israel, saying, In the tenth *day* of this month they shall take to them every man a lamb, according to the house of *their* fathers, a lamb for an house" (Exod. 12:3). God's implicit and express command was to do the following: "Draw out and take you a lamb according to your families, and kill the passover. And ye shall take a bunch of hyssop, and dip *it* in the blood that *is* in the *bason*, and strike the lintel and the two side posts with the blood that *is* in the *bason*; and none of you shall go out at the door of his house until the morning. For the LORD will pass through to smite the Egyptians; and when he seeth the blood upon the lintel, and on the two side posts, the LORD will pass over the door, and will not suffer the destroyer to come in unto your houses to smite *you*. And ye shall observe this thing for an ordinance to thee and to thy sons for ever. And it shall come to pass, when ye be come to the land which the LORD will give you, according as he hath promised, that ye shall keep this service. And it shall come to pass, when your children shall say unto you, What mean ye by this service? That ye shall say, It *is* the sacrifice of the LORD'S passover, who passed over the houses of the children of Israel in Egypt, when he smote the Egyptians, and delivered our houses. And the people bowed the head and worshipped" (Exod. 12:21–27).

All sacrifices for the atonement of committed sins, which symbolized the sacrifice to be made by Christ, were always offered by men and not by women. Abel makes the first recorded offering of a lamb in the Bible

(Gen. 4:4; Heb. 11:4). Though it is not mentioned, it is obvious that Adam must have been the first to offer the sacrificial lamb. The next sacrifice mentioned is that of Noah (Gen. 8:20). Then, there are the sacrifices of Abraham and Jacob (Gen. 22:13; 31:54). Upon the establishment of the earthly tabernacle, only men were permitted to offer sacrifices on behalf of their families (Exod. 24:5; 25:2). When women gave birth, they were to go to the door of the tabernacle with a lamb or with a young pigeon or turtledove and give them to the priest, and he would offer the burnt sacrifice for them (Exod. 12:6–8). The same was true for the purification offering after a woman's monthly cycle. They were to bring either two pigeons or two turtledoves to the door of the tabernacle, and the priest would make the sacrifice for them (Lev. 15:19–31). This continued down through the generations up to the time of David (2 Sam. 6:17), and then until the sacrificial services ended in Christ (Dan. 9:27; Matt. 27:51). Though there is no specific mention prohibiting women from making the sacrifice, the emphasis on who should do it and the thousands of years of solely male practice confirms that it was a God-given order.

There are several points to consider:

1. The Israelites were about to leave Egypt following the final judgment of God on the Egyptians.
2. To avoid the effects of the judgment about to be released upon the Egyptians, the Hebrews were to follow the precise directions God gave Moses.
3. The fathers (or elders) were the only ones instructed to place the blood on the "lintel and the two side posts." Only the men were designated to take the full responsibility for their respective homes and households.
4. The elders, or fathers, were held accountable for the salvation of their families.
5. The men were also responsible to perpetuate the practice among their families throughout their generations up to Christ.

Under God's guidance Moses was instructed through his father-in-law to put in place a system of governance to carry the responsibility of ordering the nation. "And Moses chose able men out of all Israel, and made them heads over the people, rulers of thousands, rulers of hundreds, rulers of fifties, and rulers of tens. And they judged the people at all seasons: the hard causes they brought unto Moses, but every small matter they judged themselves" (Exod. 18:25, 26). Throughout the entire Old Testament, when Israel was true to God, they followed a system with males holding the headship. However, when the nation went into apostasy, then the order that God had established changed. "*As for* my people, children *are* their oppressors, and women rule over them. O my people, they which lead thee cause *thee* to err, and destroy the way of thy paths" (Isa. 3:12).

While the words, *children* and *women* can be taken in a figurative sense in the above statement, there were times when the statement was literally true. Athaliah was one of the ones who reigned as queen in Israel, and that was for the brief period of six years after she destroyed "all the seed royal" (2 Kings 11:1, 3). When Ahab was king, it was Jezebel who actually wielded the scepter (see 1 Kings 18:13; 19:1, 2; 21:7–15). Children also ruled the people. Manasseh was twelve years old when he began to reign (2 Kings 21:1); Josiah was only eight years old when he took the scepter and was placed on the throne (2 Kings 22:1). If figurative language is intended, then the suggestion is that that which is abnormal symbolically replaced that which was supposed to be under wise male leadership. The lack of proper experienced male headship, both in the home and in society, is shamefully spoken of as a reproach to Israel. The vacuum in male headship contributed to the downfall of Israel.

God's ordained headship was again established in the New Testament church. Christ set the example, leading the church Himself and choosing twelve men to be the pillars of the New Testament order. "And he ordained twelve, that they should be with him, and that he might send them forth to preach, And to have power to heal sicknesses, and to cast out devils" (Mark 3:14, 15). He immortalized the selection of these men just before His death. "And when the hour was come, he sat down, and the twelve apostles with him. That ye may eat and drink at my table in my kingdom, and sit on thrones judging the twelve tribes of Israel" (Luke 22:14, 30). After His ascension, His apostles followed the mandate. Luke quoted Peter in describing the selection of Judas's replacement: "Beginning from the baptism of John, unto that same day that he was taken up from us, must one be ordained to be a witness with us of his resurrection" (Acts 1:22). After narrowing the eligible male candidates to two, namely "Joseph called Barsabas, who was surnamed Justus, and Matthias" (verse 23), the lot fell on "Matthias" (verse 26). Years later, Paul wrote Timothy concerning the succession of spiritual authority and leadership: "Thou therefore, my son, be strong in the grace that is in Christ Jesus. And the things that thou hast heard of me among many witnesses, the same commit thou to faithful men, who shall be able to teach others also" (2 Tim. 2:1, 2).

The New Covenant

When Christ established the New Covenant, no women were present in the Upper Room, even though there were women that followed Him to Jerusalem. "There were also women looking on afar off: among whom was Mary Magdalene, and Mary the mother of James the less and of Joses, and Salome; (who also, when he was in Galilee, followed him, and ministered unto him;) and many other women which came up with him unto Jerusalem" (Mark 15:40, 41). Besides the women there was a larger number of disciples numbering *seventy* (Luke 10:1–24). A comparison here is interesting. There were *twelve* patriarchs; there were also *twelve* disciples (cf. Rev. 7:4–8; 21:12, 14). Moses appointed *seventy* men to assist him in judging Israel (see Num. 11:16–25); Jesus also appointed *seventy* men to assist Him.

However, for this momentous occasion before His death, neither the women nor the larger group of believers were included in the ceremony, nor did the women believers participate in the establishment of the New Testament. Only the twelve men were permitted entrance into the Upper Room, and only in the hearing of the twelve men were Christ's words spoken, as Matthew declared: "Now when the even was come, he sat down with the twelve" (Matt. 26:20). Mark likewise bears witness to this fact, "And in the evening he cometh with the twelve" (Mark 14:17).

The biblical record clearly shows that the chosen men were solely included in the setting up of the New Testament church and were held responsible as leaders to insure its implementation. It was to the twelve that Jesus said in the presence of the other followers, "When the Son of man shall sit in the throne of His glory, ye also shall sit upon twelve thrones, judging the twelve tribes of Israel" (Matt. 19:28). This honored position was restated again during the Last Supper. (See Luke 22:30 below.) The record states concerning the establishment of the New Covenant: "And as they [the twelve disciples] did eat, Jesus took bread, and blessed, and brake *it*, and gave to them, and said, Take, eat: this is my body. And he took the cup, and when he had given thanks, he gave *it* to them: and they all drank of it. And he said unto them, This is my blood of the new testament, which is shed for many. Verily I say unto you, I will drink no more of the fruit of the vine, until that day that I drink it new in the kingdom of

God. And when they had sung an hymn, they went out into the mount of Olives" (Mark 14:22–26).

Luke's record also supports this: "And when the hour was come, he sat down, and the twelve apostles with him. And he said unto them, With desire I have desired to eat the passover with you before I suffer: For I say unto you, I will not any more eat thereof, until it be fulfilled in the kingdom of God. And he took the cup, and gave thanks, and said, Take this, and divide *it* among yourselves: For I say unto you, I will not drink of the fruit of the vine, until the kingdom of God shall come. And he took bread, and gave thanks, and brake *it*, and gave unto them, saying, This is my body which is given for you: this do in remembrance of me. Likewise also the cup after supper, saying, This cup *is* the new testament in my blood, which is shed for you. ... And there was also a strife among them, which of them should be accounted the greatest. And he said unto them, The kings of the Gentiles exercise lordship over them; and they that exercise authority upon them are called benefactors. But ye *shall* not *be* so: but he that is greatest among you, let him be as the younger; and he that is chief, as he that doth serve. For whether *is* greater, he that sitteth at meat, or he that serveth? *is* not he that sitteth at meat? but I am among you as he that serveth. Ye are they which have continued with me in my temptations. And I appoint unto you a kingdom, as my Father hath appointed unto me; That ye may eat and drink at my table in my kingdom, and sit on thrones judging the twelve tribes of Israel" (Luke 22:14–20, 24–30).

The book that consistently recognizes the male role bears record that, "Jesus Christ [is] the same yesterday, and to day, and for ever" (Heb. 13:8). That the twelve recognized the important role of leadership they were to exert is recorded in the book of Acts. "Then the twelve called the multitude of the disciples *unto them*, and said, It is not reason that we should leave the word of God, and serve tables. Wherefore, brethren, look ye out among you seven men of honest report, full of the Holy Ghost and wisdom, whom we may appoint over this business. But we will give ourselves continually to prayer, and to the ministry of the word" (Acts 6:2–4).

The evidence is abundant. There is a headship in God's kingdom, in His church, and in the home. Blessed are the children that are raised and nurtured in a God-ordained home, where God's love reigns in each heart and the whole family lives harmoniously under God's established order.

13.

Women Elders in the New Testament?

Though there were many women that followed Christ, when He chose His disciples, He ordained only men. "And he ordained twelve, that they should be with him, and that he might send them forth to preach, And to have power to heal sicknesses, and to cast out devils: And Simon he surnamed Peter; And James the *son* of Zebedee, and John the brother of James; and he surnamed them Boanerges, which is, The sons of thunder: And Andrew, and Philip, and Bartholomew, and Matthew, and Thomas, and James the son of Alphaeus, and Thaddaeus, and Simon the Canaanite, And Judas Iscariot, which also betrayed him: and they went into an house" (Mark 3:14–19).

There is plenty of evidence that the women on His team were numerous. "And many women were there beholding afar off, which followed Jesus from Galilee, ministering unto him: Among which was Mary Magdalene, and Mary the mother of James and Joses, and the mother of Zebedee's children" (Matt. 27:55, 56).

Among these women was Jesus' own mother. And if anybody would have met with the least amount of resistance to be elevated into a position in His church, it would have been the woman God chose to bear Christ in the virgin birth. Yet, when people attempted to place her in a privilege position, Jesus said, "Who is my mother? and who are my brethren? And he stretched forth his hand toward his disciples, and said, Behold my mother and my brethren" (Matt. 12:48, 49)! Though Christ's tender regard for Mary as His mother were made obvious at the crucifixion, yet, it is just as obvious that He did not lift her up above the men of His choosing.

The Bible also reveals that some of the women were persons of means and status. "There were also women looking on afar off: among whom was Mary Magdalene, and Mary the mother of James the less and of Joses, and Salome; (who also, when he was in Galilee, followed him, and ministered unto him;) and many other women which came up with him unto Jerusalem" (Mark 15:40, 41). "And certain women, which had been healed of evil spirits and infirmities, Mary called Magdalene, out of whom went seven devils, And Joanna the wife of Chuza Herod's steward, and Susanna, and many others, which ministered unto him of their substance" (Luke 8:2, 3). Concerning this biblical statement, the *Seventh-day Adventist Bible Commentary* states: "One of the characteristics of the Gospel of Luke is its frequent references to Christ's ministry for the womenfolk of Palestine and the ministry of some of them on His behalf. This was something new, for the role of Jewish women in public life had been a relatively minor one, although in isolated instances, prophets like Elisha had ministered to women and been ministered to by them."[58] With regard to Chuza, the commentary further states: "Nothing further is known of this man. A steward held a position of no mean importance in the household he served (see on Matt. 20:8)."[59] Regarding Joanna, the commentary states: "Being the wife of Herod's steward, she must have been a person of wealth and influence."[60]

Since she was a woman of high caliber and was financially established, it would have been reasonable for Christ to have elevated her to the role of apostleship. Yet, He did not.

When it came to supporting Christ in going through with His sacrifice, two humans were sent. "And there appeared unto them Elias with Moses: and they were talking with Jesus" (Mark 9:4). We might consider that, though there were women prophetesses in the Old Testament, such as Miriam (Exod. 15:20), Deborah (Judges 4:4), and Huldah (2 Kings 22:14), none is mentioned as having been elevated to the position of these men. Neither were women chosen to consult with Jesus over the destiny of humankind.

Just as Christ began His earthly ministry selecting men to take up the responsibility of the church, so did He bring that ministry to a close. The fact that none of the seventy outside the twelve were mentioned in the episode of the Last Supper suggests a very important point. In Matthew 26:19 and 20 we read: "And the disciples did as Jesus had appointed them; and they made ready the passover. Now when the even was come, he sat down with the twelve." Here is an intentional exclusivity. Christ

58 Commenting on Luke 8:2, *The Seventh-day Adventist Bible Commentary*, vol. 5, p. 769.
59 Commenting on Luke 8:3, *The Seventh-day Adventist Bible Commentary*, vol. 5, p. 770.
60 Commenting on Luke 8:3, *The Seventh-day Adventist Bible Commentary*, vol. 5, p. 770.

permitted none but the twelve to share the Last Supper with Him. Only twelve men partook of the sacred emblems. And it was to these twelve that Christ said, "Verily I say unto you, That ye which have followed me, in the regeneration when the Son of man shall sit in the throne of his glory, ye also shall sit upon twelve thrones, judging the twelve tribes of Israel" (Matt. 19:28).

According to the book of Hebrews, everything intended by the Savior to be implemented into the New Testament had to be put in place prior to His death. Paul wrote, "For where a testament is, there must also of necessity be the death of the testator. For a testament is of force after men are dead: otherwise it is of no strength at all while the testator liveth" (Heb. 9:16, 17). Therefore, had Christ intended to place women in church leadership, He could have very well introduced them in this pivotal introduction of the New Testament. But, He did not.

In the Upper Room, the believers gathered together after the Crucifixion weekend. "And when they were come in, they went up into an upper room, where abode both Peter, and James, and John, and Andrew, Philip, and Thomas, Bartholomew, and Matthew, James *the son* of Alphaeus, and Simon Zelotes, and Judas *the brother* of James. These all continued with one accord in prayer and supplication, with the women, and Mary the mother of Jesus, and with his brethren" (Acts 1:13, 14). During this convocation an important issue arose.

> *According to the book of Hebrews, everything intended by the Savior to be implemented into the New Testament had to be put in place prior to His death.*

Peter declared: "Men *and* brethren, this scripture must needs have been fulfilled, which the Holy Ghost by the mouth of David spake before concerning Judas, which was guide to them that took Jesus. For he was numbered with us, and had obtained part of this ministry. Now this man purchased a field with the reward of iniquity; and falling headlong, he burst asunder in the midst, and all his bowels gushed out. And it was known unto all the dwellers at Jerusalem; insomuch as that field is called in their proper tongue, Aceldama, that is to say, The field of blood. For it is written in the book of Psalms, Let his habitation be desolate, and let no man dwell therein: and his bishoprick let another take. Wherefore of these men which have companied with us all the time that the Lord Jesus went in and out among us, Beginning from the baptism of John, unto that same day that he was taken up from us, must one be ordained to be a witness with us of his resurrection. And they appointed two, Joseph called Barsabas, who was surnamed Justus, and Matthias. And they prayed, and said, Thou, Lord, which knowest the hearts of all *men*, shew whether of these two thou hast chosen, That he may take part of this ministry and apostleship, from which Judas by transgression fell, that he might go to his own place. And they gave forth their lots; and the lot fell upon Matthias; and he was numbered with the eleven apostles" (Acts 1:16–26).

No one can doubt that the Holy Spirit had taken charge of Peter and enlightened him concerning this rather important matter. Here was an opportunity for the New Testament church to be introduced to a new development. An apostolic position had just been recently vacated. Here was the perfect time to place one of the prominent women in this spot. But, though there were many devout women in the Upper Room, when it came to replacing the fallen disciple, the Spirit led the leaders to select a man.

In the fourth chapter of Revelation, God shows John twenty-four thrones before the throne of God. "And round about the throne *were* four and twenty seats: and upon the seats I saw four and twenty elders sitting, clothed in white raiment; and they had on their heads crowns of gold" (Rev. 4:4). The word "*elder*" is translated from the Greek word *presbuteros*. It is used seventy-two times in the New Testament, of which fifty-seven times it is translated "elder." The connotation is in reference to a man holding a position in the church like a pastor or another church leader. Ten times it is translated "older man." This meaning assumes the quality of old age. Today we use the terms "senior" and "elderly" to mean a wise person (man or woman) of advanced age, presupposing wisdom comes with age. In other words, part of the reason they are leaders is because of the wisdom and spiritual maturity they have gotten through life.

Only once is the word translated "elder women" (1 Tim. 5:2). In that case, Paul is contrasting older men with older women, and younger men with younger women, and the apostle is simply making sure that the senior women are treated with respect and that the younger women are dealt with in purity.

Thus, the evidence suggests that the twenty-four elders are men of long experience with the Lord who have been redeemed from the earth.

The apostle Paul used the terms *"episkopos"* and *"presbuteros"* when refer-ring to men in leadership. In Acts 20:17–28, as he was nearing the end of his ministry, he gave a final word of exhortation to the church in Ephesus. In verse 17, he addressed the *presbuteros* (elders) of the church. In verse 28, he referred to these same men as *episkopos*, or "overseers." In describ-ing the same group one time as *presbuteros* and a second time as *episkopos*, Paul seems to have considered the two words to be synonyms for men in the role of church leaders.

In Titus 1:5, Paul wrote Titus to remind him that he left him in Crete with instructions to appoint *presbuteros* (i.e., elders) over the churches in every city. To Paul, an elder is clearly a position of leadership over a church. In verse 7, Paul begins describing the qualifications for an elder using the word *episkopos* (i.e., bishop) to describe this same group. Once again, Paul seems to use these two words for mature male leaders interchangeably.

My conclusion in all of this is to reiterate that the term "elder," which, biblically speaking, is masculine in nature, never refers to a woman hold-ing "elder" as a title. Even during Moses' lifespan, when it was time to select people who would take part of Moses' burdens, the Lord directed the choice to be men. "The Lord directed Moses to gather before him seventy of the elders, whom he knew to be the elders of the people. They were not to be those only in advanced years, but men of dignity, sound judgment, and experience, who were qualified to be judges, or officers. 'And bring them unto the tabernacle of the congregation, that they may stand there with thee. And I will come down and talk with thee there; and I will take of the spirit which is upon thee, and will put it upon them, and they shall bear the burden of the people with thee, that thou bear it not thyself alone. ...' " (*Spiritual Gifts*, vol. 4a, p. 16).

In reading through Mrs. White's writings, I have discovered the same usage as the Bible. She uses the term "elder" exclusively for men. For example, she wrote, "It is quite possible that elders Jones and Waggoner ..."[61] In another place she wrote, "In company with Elders Whitney and Conradi ..."[62] When referring to a particular man and his spouse, she wrote, "Elder and Mrs. Haskell were conducting Bible studies."[63]

Some suggest that the issue was cultural. "In those biblical days," they say, "women were held below the status of men." However, though this was

---

61 E. G. White, *Manuscript Release*, vol. 3, p. 201.
62 E. G. White, *Manuscript Release*, vol. 3, p. 393.
63 E. G. White, *Review and Herald*, Nov. 29, 1906.

> **The heathen had subjugated their women to positions even lower than the Israelites. And yet, they had women priestesses, while the Israelites only permitted priestesses when they were in a state of apostasy.**

at times true in Israel when they had abandoned or renounced their religious beliefs (Judges 20), the heathen had subjugated their women to positions even lower than the Israelites. And yet, they had women priestesses, while the Israelites only permitted priestesses when they were in a state of apostasy. The most infamous of such priestesses was Jezebel who practiced witchcraft (2 Kings 9:22; Rev. 2:20). But be it far from God's faithful people to retreat to the practices that contributed to ancient Israel's decline and final ruin.

14.

Chauvinism or Godly Order

Supporters of women becoming pastors argue that chauvinism and the desire to control are the chief motivating factors of those who are against women becoming pastors. And while it is true that chauvinists do abound who feel obliged to suppress their wives and other women, latching onto Paul's words, "Wives, submit yourselves unto your own husbands" (Col. 3:18), and they misuse his statements, it is also true that they do so without due consideration for the qualifying words, "as it is fit in the Lord" (Col. 3:18). This particular submissive characteristic was enjoined upon all Christians, including men. "Obey them that have the rule over you, and submit yourselves: for they watch for your souls, as they that must give account, that they may do it with joy, and not with grief: for that is unprofitable for you" (Heb. 13:17). "Submit yourselves therefore to God. Resist the devil, and he will flee from you" (James 4:7). "Submit yourselves to every ordinance of man for the Lord's sake: whether it be to the king, as supreme" (1 Peter 2:13). "Likewise, ye younger, submit yourselves unto the elder. Yea, all *of you* be subject one to another, and be clothed with humility: for God resisteth the proud, and giveth grace to the humble" (1 Peter 5:5). Submissiveness is a characteristic of our Lord. Jesus said, "I delight to do thy will, O my God: yea, thy law *is* within my heart" (Ps. 40:8).

But this characteristic is challenging to the one who is determined to have his or her own way. To such a person, "Blessed are the meek" is an unwanted quality. They can therefore confuse leading with controlling. To teach my daughter how to ride a bicycle, I had to steer until I was certain that she could safely ride on her own. Her trust in me led her to see a loving father looking out for her well-being, and the resulting safety provided the free exercise of joy. Christ created this earth and entrusted it to the stewardship of Adam (Gen. 1:26–28). But in no way did the Lord stop steering. While He does not take man's freedom of choice away, it does not mean that He stops managing. True Christians are not Deists. By the prohibition to avoid eating the fruit from the tree of knowledge of good and evil, God placed man on probation. The happy estate of Adam and Eve could be kept solely on the condition of submission and loyalty to the Creator's will. They could obey and live, or they could disobey and die.

The term "probation" means the process or period of testing or observing the character or abilities of a person in a certain role that someone supervises. Adam's fall demanded more supervision then in his pre-fallen condition. Freedom of choice in God's kingdom has positive constraints. Willing conformity and obedience to God's revealed will is true liberty. The Lord is a God of order, and He tells His children: "If ye will obey my voice indeed, and keep my covenant, then ye shall be a peculiar treasure to me above all people: for all the earth *is* mine" (Exod. 19:5). That is His desire. Liberty does not mean permissiveness. "For this is the love of God, that we keep his commandments: and his commandments are not grievous" (1 John 5:3).

The 1960s were very difficult and turbulent times in American history. The draft dodging, flag burning, and unrestrained upheavals during the hippy movement were nothing more than a protest against formalism, society's standards, conventionalism, and structured normalcy. Young people sought to cast off all restraint and to adopt a lifestyle free from rules, laws, or anything that had a tinge of order. I was one of them. That there was need for reforms, there is no question. But the outcome of this movement ended in complete mayhem and chaos. There was irreversible brain damage and irretrievable abandonment of values as individuals were deceived into accepting a surreal existence through LSD in place of the reality that life has to have structure if it is to continue to exist. Following that model would have left American society lawless, with a lack of order, and without restraint and morals. This would have been the overall state of things had this so-called freedom been permitted to thrive to any significant degree.

Church Control?

The church has been vested with the duty of guarding biblical truths and standards. "The church of the living God" is "the pillar and ground of the truth" (1 Tim. 3:15). Both the disobedient and those with supposed new light consider the church's authority to be intrusive and restrictive popery. Remember Jesus' counsel to the church in Matthew 18:15–17. In God's church, no one has unrestrictive liberty to do as he or she pleases. The inspired counsel of Paul says: "Dare any of you, having a matter against another, go to law before the unjust, and not before the saints? Do ye not know that the saints shall judge the world? and if the world shall be judged by you, are ye unworthy to judge the smallest matters? Know ye not that we shall judge angels? how much more things that pertain to this life? If then ye have judgments of things pertaining to this life, set them to judge who are least esteemed in the church. I speak to your shame. Is it so, that there is not a wise man among you? no, not one that shall be able to judge between his brethren? But brother goeth to law with brother, and that before the unbelievers. Now therefore there is utterly a fault among you, because ye go to law one with another. Why do ye not rather take wrong? why do ye not rather *suffer yourselves to* be defrauded? Nay, ye do wrong, and defraud, and that *your* brethren. Know ye not that the unrighteous shall not inherit the kingdom of God? Be not deceived: neither fornicators, nor idolaters, nor adulterers, nor effeminate, nor abusers of themselves with mankind, Nor thieves, nor covetous, nor drunkards, nor revilers, nor extortioners, shall inherit the kingdom of God. And such were some of you: but ye are washed, but ye are sanctified, but ye are justified in the name of the Lord Jesus, and by the Spirit of our God" (1 Cor. 6:1–11). "For God is not *the author* of confusion, but of peace, as in all churches of the saints. ... If any man think himself to be a prophet, or spiritual, let him acknowledge that the things that I write unto you are the commandments of the Lord. ... Let all things be done decently and in order" (1 Cor. 14:33, 37, 40). "If any man obey not our word by this epistle, note that man, and have no company with him, that he may be ashamed. Yet count *him* not as an enemy, but admonish *him* as a brother" (2 Thess. 3:14, 15).

One of the church's responsibilities is to limit people from overstepping the bounds of God's ordained roles. That goes for men as well as for women. Because God is a God of order, everything connected with Heaven must also be in perfect order. Thorough discipline and subjection mark the movements of the angelic host. There are cherubim and seraphim. Order and harmonious action are the means of attaining success in God's kingdom. Therefore, God requires order and system in His work no less in today's church than in the day of the church in the wilderness (Acts 7:38) and in the apostolic church (1 Cor. 14:40). God also expects Christians to adhere to civil authority. "Let every soul be subject unto the higher powers. For there is no power but of God: the powers that be are ordained of God. Whosoever therefore resisteth the power, resisteth the ordinance of God: and they that resist shall receive to themselves damnation. For rulers are not a terror to good works, but to the evil. Wilt thou then not be afraid of the power? do that which is good, and thou shalt have praise of the same: For he is the minister of God to thee for good. But if thou do that which is evil, be afraid; for he beareth not the sword in vain: for he is the minister of God, a revenger to *execute* wrath upon him that doeth evil" (Rom. 13:1–4).

> **One of the church's responsibilities is to limit people from overstepping the bounds of God's ordained roles. That goes for men as well as for women.**

None who believes that Christ is Lord can presuppose that liberty should be without self-restraint or restraint toward others, for Christ left specific instructions on how to redemptively handle a believer who is disorderly, either doctrinally or morally. He counseled: "Moreover if thy brother shall trespass against thee, go and tell him his fault between thee and him alone: if he shall hear thee, thou hast gained thy brother. But if he will not hear *thee, then* take with thee one or two more, that in the mouth of two or three witnesses every word may be established. And if he shall neglect to hear them, tell *it* unto the church: but if he neglect to hear the church, let him be unto thee as an heathen man and a publican. Verily I say unto you, Whatsoever ye shall bind on earth shall be bound in heaven: and whatsoever ye shall loose on earth shall be loosed in heaven" (Matt. 18:15–18).

Request for "Variance"

A state of affairs during the period of the Old Testament reveals a condition that is now suggested as a solution for the church. But "every man did *that which was* right in his own eyes" (Judges 21:25). It was God who led the church in the wilderness, put in place a spiritual male leadership, and established a form of government to manage the people. The same is true of the New Testament church. Discipline and order were essential for the success of the Christian church. And the same is true today. To allow for unbiblical practices in any segment of the church is to create confusion. The Bible's admonition is: "Now I beseech you, brethren, by the name of our Lord Jesus Christ, that ye all speak the same thing, and *that* there be no divisions among you; but *that* ye be perfectly joined together in the same mind and in the same judgment" (1 Cor. 1:10). Departing from a male led ministry will not unite the church. Instead, such a departure has and will encourage theological pluralism and regionalization.

No Women Pastors in the Bible

It is true that, in the Scriptures, there are words that are *epicene*—which means that they are neuter or sexless in nature. Such words can be applied to both male and female. Examples of such words are "teacher" (Hab. 2:18; Rom. 2:20) and "cousin," as in the case of Elizabeth (Luke 1:36). On the other hand, the word "shepherd" is always non-epicene, that is, it is rather masculine in gender. With this fact in mind, a scholar who spoke with me one time stated, "Rachel, the wife of Jacob, was a pastor because she was a shepherd. Since the word 'shepherd' is masculine, then she was a pastor."

After that unusual encounter, I decided to check out his assertion. My research did not bear out his conclusion. What I found was the verse, "Rachel came with her father's sheep: for she kept them" (Gen. 29:9). And while it is true that she kept the sheep, the Bible does not call her a shepherd. Moreover, if it requires no qualification to make anyone who carries the title "shepherd" a pastor, then all of Jacob's sons were pastors (Gen. 46:34). Also, the mean shepherds that Moses had to fight off for mistreating Jethro's daughters were also pastors, and the daughters themselves likewise were pastors (Exod. 2:16–21). Then too the shepherds waiting for the stone to be moved as Rachel showed up (Gen. 29:3–10) were also pastors, as were the shepherds that David protected (1 Sam. 25:7), Cyrus (Isa. 44:28), idol shepherds (Zech. 11:17), and the shepherds abiding in the fields during Christ's birth (Luke 2:8, 15). All were pastors. But is that right?

Can we not see the faulty logic herein applied? No, there is no biblical record of any woman priest or pastor. Though the word "shepherd" is in the male gender, there were times in a family that there were no sons, so, consequently, the daughters or wives had to carry the load and do the job of tending to the flocks. To suggest that Rachel was a pastor because she "kept the sheep" to be able to establish a biblical example, or precedent, for ordaining female pastors falls seriously short of correct biblical interpretation. It is a serious departure from proper biblical exegesis. As we have noted, the only woman "priest" (for the word "priestess" does not appear in the Bible) to come from among God's people was Jezebel, daughter of the high priest of Baal (2 Kings 9:22; Rev. 2:20). She comes the closes to being a "priest," but no true believer would ever want to follow her example.

Equality

In salvation, men and women are equal. Yet, by virtue of their creation, as has already been discussed, they are different and not meant to be compared. Though both human, in all other matters they are not the same. Four American quarters are equal in value to a dollar bill, but the coins and the bill are not the same. They have different functions. Equal does not equate to being the same. Though some use the text, "There is neither Jew nor Greek, there is neither bond nor free, there is neither male nor female: for ye are all one in Christ Jesus" (Gal. 3:28), to suggest that God did away with gender, race, etc., such a conclusion is not substantiated in the New Testament. The stress in the text is *unity* and *equality* in faith and salvation, not sameness. A man is still a man, and a woman is still a woman; a Jew is still a Jew, and a Greek is still a Greek. Christ did not come to change the race, color, gender, or nationality of a person. He came to offer salvation and a change of heart to all.

Compromise for the Sake of Peace and Unity

Christ's prayer for oneness was based on the Scriptures (John 17:11–21). Truth cannot be compromised on the altar of peace or of unity. Christ's own words, "Think not that I am come to send peace on earth: I came not to send peace, but a sword" (Matt. 10:34), should set at rest any such notion. For the sake of unity and peace, the Roman emperor Constantine introduced worldly practices into the church, resulting in the watering down of the truth and the opening of the way for the rise of the mystical women of Revelation, with the more than 41,000 different Christian denominations in existence today. Concession to non-biblical practices and teachings is not a biblical basis for unity and peace. The warnings in the Scriptures are too clear to disregard. "If there arise among you a prophet, or a dreamer of dreams, and giveth thee a sign or a wonder, And the sign or the wonder come to pass, whereof he spake unto thee, saying, Let us go after other gods, which thou hast not known, and let us serve them; Thou shalt not hearken unto the words of that prophet, or that dreamer of dreams: for the LORD your God proveth you, to know whether ye love the LORD your God with all your heart and with all your soul. Ye shall walk after the LORD your God, and fear him, and keep his commandments, and obey his voice, and ye shall serve him, and cleave unto him" (Deut. 13:1–4).

Paul, the great defender of the Christian faith, wrote: "I marvel that ye are so soon removed from him that called you into the grace of Christ unto another gospel: Which is not another; but there be some that trouble you, and would pervert the gospel of Christ. But though we, or an angel from heaven, preach any other gospel unto you than that which we have preached unto you, let him be accursed. As we said before, so say I now again, If any *man* preach any other gospel unto you than that ye have received, let him be accursed" (Gal. 1:6–9; "man" is supplied). And the longest living apostle still carrying the burden of the purity of the truth warned: "If there come any unto you, and bring not this doctrine, receive him not into *your* house, neither bid him God speed: For he that biddeth him God speed is partaker of his evil deeds" (2 John 10, 11). Also, Jude's words suggest that there was a life-and-death struggle over the Christian faith. He wrote: "Beloved, when I gave all diligence to write unto you of the common salvation, it was needful for me to write unto you, and exhort you that ye should earnestly contend for the faith which was once delivered unto the saints" (Jude 3). Christ neither bartered nor negotiated biblical truths; neither should a genuine Christian.

Gender Blending

God's displeasure concerning gender blending or erasing the differences between the sexes is clearly outlined in the Scriptures. Here is what it says: "The woman shall not wear that which pertaineth unto a man, neither shall a man put on a woman's garment: for all that do so *are* abomination unto the LORD thy God" (Deut. 22:5). "Thou shalt not lie with mankind, as with womankind: it is abomination" (Lev. 18:22). In every culture, nature has dictated a variance between how females and males act and dress. When it comes to morality, the Lord defines quite well the lines relative to gender. He commanded: "If a man also lie with mankind, as he lieth with a woman, both of them have committed an abomination: they shall surely be put to death; their blood shall be upon them" (Lev. 20:13). "For this cause God gave them up unto vile affections: for even their women did change the natural use into that which is against nature: And likewise also the men, leaving the natural use of the woman, burned in their lust one toward another; men with men working that which is unseemly, and receiving in themselves that recompense of their error which was meet. And even as they did not like to retain God in *their* knowledge, God gave them over to a reprobate mind, to do those things which are not convenient" (Rom. 1:26–28). "Know ye not that the unrighteous shall not inherit the kingdom of God? Be not deceived: neither fornicators, nor idolaters, nor adulterers, nor effeminate, nor abusers of themselves with mankind" (1 Cor. 6:9). "For whoremongers, for them that defile themselves with mankind, for menstealers, for liars, for perjured persons, and if there be any other thing that is contrary to sound doctrine" (1 Tim. 1:10).

In the beginning, when God ordained marriage, He said, "Therefore shall a man leave his father and his mother, and shall cleave unto his wife: and they shall be one flesh" (Gen. 2:24). Four thousand years later, He affirmed the same in Matthew 19:4–6. "And he answered and said unto them, Have ye not read, that he which made *them* at the beginning made them male and female, And said, For this cause shall a man leave father and mother, and shall cleave to his wife: and they twain shall be one flesh? Wherefore they are no more twain, but one flesh. What therefore God hath joined together, let not man put asunder." It is crystal clear that the wife was a woman and the man was her husband in Genesis and that same arrangement continued in the days of Christ. Therefore, the lack of gender differentiation today is opening the door to society's acceptance of same sex relationships, marriages, and gender confusion. This is clear evidence that society is regressing to the moral decadence of the days of Noah and of the days of Sodom and Gomorrah.

Judgmental

Some writers say that God's character of grace and love precludes judgment. Now, while it is true that we should not be judgmental, for we do not know what motivates another person's every act, we nonetheless must be able to judge between right and wrong, between truth and error. Otherwise, we would not be able to know what truth is. (See Acts 4:19; 1 Cor. 2:14, 15.) A Christ-like spirit, however, does not mean one has to accept error, nor does it mean that a non-biblical practice should be countenanced or tolerated. While it is true that God forgave Adam and Eve, it is also true that He put them out of the garden (Gen. 3:22–24). There are times when God expected and still expects His people to distinguish between that which is wrong and that which is right. Christ plainly warned the leaders of His day concerning false teachings: "But in vain they do worship me, teaching *for* doctrines the commandments of men" (Matt. 15:9). The same was true for Paul. He wrote: "As I besought thee to abide still at Ephesus, when I went into Macedonia, that thou mightest charge some that they teach no other doctrine" (1 Tim. 1:3). Being able to detect the rightness of a practice or teaching is not being judgmental. Rather, it is exercising good judgment.

Cultural

The word "culture" does not exist in the Bible. The Bible writers used the words *"traditions"* and *"customs"* (Matt. 15:2, 3, 6; Mark 7:3–13; Acts 28:17; Col. 2:8; 1 Pet. 1:18). Today, *culture*, with its elevating tone, is a word that is used to substitute for the biblical words. When people make this substitution, it suggests that all customs and practices are now acceptable. However, from Christ's own words, relevance and culture should not dictate our beliefs.

Jesus, who is our loving Savior, Redeemer, and Mediator—in short, everything to us—left us with the counsel of the following words: "Enter ye in at the strait gate: for wide *is* the gate, and broad *is* the way, that leadeth to destruction, and many there be which go in thereat: Because strait *is* the gate, and narrow *is* the way, which leadeth unto life, and few there be that find it" (Matt. 7:13, 14). "Howbeit in vain do they worship me, teaching for doctrines the commandments of men. For laying aside the commandment of God, ye hold the tradition of men" (Mark 7:7, 8). Christ denounced traditions that caused their adherents to violate the principles, teachings, and practices enjoined upon the believers through the Scriptures. If He had come to support the traditions of men, He could have well presented Himself to the Samaritan woman at the well dressed like a Samaritan. But He didn't. Read the story in John 4:5–26. She was obviously sectarian in her thinking and tried to use her culture to segregate herself from Christ. But Christ did not mix words. He let her know that neither her culture nor the culture of the Jews was of any value when it came to worship and salvation. If He stood so strongly about how people used cultures to diminish His teachings then, how much more strongly would He rebuke those who insist that some apparently cultural statement in the Bible lessens the inspiration of the Scriptures.

"The follower of Christ will meet with the 'enticing words' against which the apostle warned the Colossian believers. He will meet with spiritualistic interpretations of the Scriptures, but he is not to accept them.

His voice is to be heard in clear affirmation of the eternal truths of the Scriptures. Keeping his eyes fixed on Christ, he is to move steadily forward in the path marked out, discarding all ideas that are not in harmony with His teaching. The truth of God is to be the subject for his contemplation and meditation. He is to regard the Bible as the voice of God speaking directly to him. Thus he will find the wisdom which is divine" (*The Acts of the Apostles*, pp. 474, 475).

God Gave Israel a King Against His Wishes

Some argue that, since God permitted Israel to have a king, even though He did not want them to have one, why would He not do the same today and accept women pastors. This argument is based on 1 Samuel 8:4–18. However, in the tone of God's response to the people's call for a king, it is obvious that God considered the people's demand a rejection not of the prophet but of Himself and His authority. "Then all the elders of Israel gathered themselves together, and came to Samuel unto Ramah, And said unto him, Behold, thou art old, and thy sons walk not in thy ways: now make us a king to judge us like all the nations. But the thing displeased Samuel, when they said, Give us a king to judge us. And Samuel prayed unto the LORD. And the LORD said unto Samuel, Hearken unto the voice of the people in all that they say unto thee: for they have not rejected thee, but they have rejected me, that I should not reign over them. According to all the works which they have done since the day that I brought them up out of Egypt even unto this day, wherewith they have forsaken me, and served other gods, so do they also unto thee. Now therefore hearken unto their voice: howbeit yet protest solemnly unto them, and shew them the manner of the king that shall reign over them. And Samuel told all the words of the LORD unto the people that asked of him a king. And he said, This will be the manner of the king that shall reign over you" (1 Sam. 8:4–11). After Samuel clarified the evil consequences of their demand (see verses 11–18), the people responded: "Nay; but we will have a king over us; That we also may be like all the nations; and that our king may judge us, and go out before us, and fight our battles" (verses 19, 20).

It is inconceivable that any true Christian would choose to apply this example as a rationale for ordaining women pastors. Anyone actually reading the complete story should be able to see in it a plain blatant spirit of anarchy and rebellion. In Hosea 13:11, God says, "I gave thee a king in mine anger, and took him away in my wrath." In view of this, why would any God-loving and God-fearing person want to tempt the Lord? Selecting a king to emulate worldly policies and practices contributed to the rise, fall, and annihilation of Israel as a nation and a people. Choosing to make a woman a pastor because God gave Israel a king against His wishes is asking for the same consequences that resulted from their faulty choice. It is written of Israel that God "rained flesh also upon them as dust, and feathered fowls like as the sand of the sea: And he let *it* fall in the midst of their camp, round about their habitations. So they did eat, and were well filled: for he gave them their own desire; They were not estranged from their lust. But while their meat was yet in their mouths, The wrath of God came upon them, and slew the fattest of them, and smote down the chosen men of Israel" (Ps. 78:27–31). Their demands to force the hand of God and then act as if it was His will only brought them disaster. The only safe path for a believer is to seek to be in harmony with His revealed will instead of finding a loophole in His will.

15.

Strange Anomalies Still Practiced

There are several anomalies (deviations from the standard) in practice among the people mentioned in Jeremiah's writings that contributed to their downfall. One in particular has to do with the subject at hand. Normally, in Jewish worship, priests were solely responsible for offering sacrifices and burning incense on behalf of themselves, their families, and the people. Their brethren, who were also Levites, took care of other services of the tabernacle of the house of God. "But Aaron and his sons **offered upon the altar of the burnt offering, and on the altar of incense**, *and were appointed* for all the work of the *place* most holy, and to make an atonement for Israel, according to all that Moses the servant of God had commanded" (1 Chron. 6:49, emphasis supplied).

But by the time that Judah was suffering terrible defeats under the Babylonians, causing the Jews to scatter, God revealed a causative element contributing to their demise as a nation. Jeremiah tells them: "Have ye forgotten the wickedness of your fathers, and the wickedness of the kings of Judah, and the wickedness of their wives, and your own wickedness, and the wickedness of your wives, which they have committed in the land of Judah, and in the streets of Jerusalem? They are not humbled *even* unto this day, neither have they feared, nor walked in my law, nor in my statutes, that I set before you and before your fathers. Therefore thus saith the LORD of hosts, the God of Israel; Behold, I will set my face against you for evil, and to cut off all Judah. And I will take the remnant of Judah, that have set their faces to go into the land of Egypt to sojourn there, and they shall all be consumed, *and* fall in the land of Egypt; they shall *even* be consumed by the sword *and* by the famine: they shall die, from the least even unto the greatest, by the sword and by the famine: and they shall be an execration, *and* an astonishment, and a curse, and a reproach. For I will punish them that dwell in the land of Egypt, as I have punished Jerusalem, by the sword, by the famine, and by the pestilence" (Jer. 44:9–13).

What was it that the wives of the kings and the other wives did that God considered wickedness? These royal women encouraged apostasy through their example and practices, and their strong influence can be traced quite amply in the history of God's people. Solomon introduced idolatry largely through the influence of his heathen wives. "For it came to pass, when Solomon was old, *that* his wives turned away his heart after other gods: and his heart was not perfect with the LORD his God, as *was* the heart of David his father. For Solomon went after Ashtoreth the goddess of the Zidonians, and after Milcom the abomination of the Ammonites. And Solomon did evil in the sight of the LORD, and went not fully after the LORD, as *did* David his father. Then did Solomon build an high place for Chemosh, the abomination of Moab, in the hill that *is* before Jerusalem, and for Molech, the abomination of the children of Ammon. And likewise did he for all his strange wives, which burnt incense and sacrificed unto their gods" (1 Kings 11:4–8). Another one was the queen mother of Asa: "And also Maachah his mother, even her he removed from *being* queen, because she had made an idol in a grove; and Asa destroyed her idol, and burnt *it* by the brook Kidron" (1 Kings 15:13). The same was true of the queen mother of Ahaziah, who exerted the same wicked influence over Israel. "Forty and two years old *was* Ahaziah when he began to reign, and he reigned one year in Jerusalem. His mother's name also *was* Athaliah the daughter of Omri. He also walked in the ways of the house of Ahab: for his mother was his counsellor to do wickedly" (2 Chron. 22:2, 3). Many royal women of Judah were of foreign birth, and, therefore, became the chief promoters of alien idol worship among the wives of the nobles and the other citizens who followed their iniquitous example.

By the time of Jeremiah, the women's influence over the men and the men's countenancing the practices of idol worship had become unabashed. "Then all the men which knew that their wives had burned incense unto other gods, and all the women that stood by, a great multitude, even all the people that dwelt in the land of Egypt, in Pathros, answered Jeremiah, saying, *As for* the word that thou hast spoken unto us in the name of the LORD, we will not hearken unto thee. But we will certainly do whatsoever thing goeth forth out of our own mouth, to burn incense unto the queen of heaven, and to pour out drink offerings unto her, as we have done, we, and our fathers, our kings, and our princes, in the cities of Judah, and in the streets of Jerusalem: for *then* had we plenty of victuals, and were well, and saw no evil. But since we left off to burn incense to the queen of heaven, and to pour out drink offerings unto her, we have wanted all *things*, and have been consumed by the sword and by the famine. And when we burned incense to the queen of heaven, and poured out drink offerings unto her, did we make her cakes to worship her, and pour out drink offerings unto her, without our men" ((Jer. 44:15–19).

These women were participating in and performing the rites of the priests. Even though people used aromatic gums, perfumes, and myrrh for weddings, on beds, and to honor people (see Ps. 45:8; Prov. 7:17; 27:9; Song of Solomon 3:6), according to God's prohibitions, no one but priests from the seed of Aaron were allowed to burn incense (1 Sam. 2:28; contrast Jer. 44:19). Everyone but Aaron and his male descendants were prohibited from offering incense. Not even kings were permitted to offer incense in the temple. King Uzziah's attempt to offer incense in the temple was met with swift retribution. "But when he was strong, his heart was lifted up to *his* destruction: for he transgressed against the LORD his God, and went into the temple of the LORD to burn incense upon the altar of incense. And Azariah the priest went in after him, and with him fourscore priests of the LORD, *that were* valiant men: And they withstood Uzziah the king, and said unto him, *It appertaineth* not unto thee, Uzziah, to burn incense unto the LORD, but to the priests the sons of Aaron, that are consecrated to burn incense: go out of the sanctuary; for thou hast trespassed; neither *shall it be* for thine honour from the LORD God. Then Uzziah was wroth, and *had* a censer in his hand to burn incense: and while he was wroth with the priests, the leprosy even rose up in his forehead before the priests in the house of the LORD, from beside the incense altar. And Azariah the chief priest, and all the priests, looked upon him, and, behold, he *was* leprous in his forehead, and they thrust him out from thence; yea, himself hasted also to go out, because the LORD had smitten him. And Uzziah the king was a leper unto the day of his death, and dwelt in a several house, *being* a leper; for he was cut off from the house of the LORD: and Jotham his son *was* over the king's house, judging the people of the land" (2 Chron. 26:16–21). Though this dreadful example was well known, these women disregarded the admonition.

Responding to their unabashedly insolent acts of sacrilege, Jeremiah declared: "The incense that ye burned in the cities of Judah, and in the streets of Jerusalem, ye, and your fathers, your kings, and your princes, and the people of the land, did not the LORD remember them, and came it *not* into his mind? So that the LORD could no longer bear, because of the evil of your doings, *and* because of the abominations which ye have committed; therefore is your land a desolation, and an astonishment, and a curse, without an inhabitant, as at this day. Because ye have burned incense, and because ye have sinned against the LORD, and have not obeyed the voice of the LORD, nor walked in his law, nor in his statutes, nor in his testimonies; therefore this evil is happened unto you, as at this day. Moreover Jeremiah said unto all the people, and to all the women, Hear the word of the LORD, all Judah that *are* in the land of Egypt: Thus saith the LORD of hosts, the God of Israel, saying; Ye and your wives have both spoken with your mouths, and fulfilled with your hand, saying, We will surely perform our vows that we have vowed, to burn incense to the queen of heaven, and to pour out drink offerings unto her: ye will surely accomplish your vows, and surely perform your vows" (Jer. 44:21–26).

Concerning the offering of incense, the command from Jehovah was: "And thou shalt make an altar to burn incense upon: *of* shittim wood shalt thou make it. ... And Aaron shall burn thereon sweet incense every morning: when he dresseth the lamps, he shall burn incense upon it. And when Aaron lighteth the lamps at even, he shall burn incense upon it, a perpetual incense before the LORD throughout your gener-ations" (Exod. 30:1, 7, 8). King Hezekiah had a perfect understanding relative to this restriction. Speaking to the priests, he said: "My sons, be not now negligent: for the LORD hath chosen you to stand before him, to serve him, and that ye should minister unto him, and burn incense" (2 Chron. 29:11).

In the contest concerning who could be a priest, Korah the Levite and the 250 princes used censers to offer incense as proof of their right to the priesthood. Responding to their afront, Moses told them: "Even to morrow the LORD will shew who *are* his, and who is holy; and will cause him to come near unto him: even *him* whom he hath chosen will he cause to come near unto him. This do; Take you censers, Korah, and all his company; and put fire therein, and put incense in them before the LORD to morrow: and it shall be *that* the man whom the LORD doth choose, he *shall be* holy" (Num. 16:5, 6). When they showed up the next morning with their censers, the results were that "there came out a fire from the LORD, and consumed the two hundred and fifty men that offered incense" (Num. 16:35). The purpose for this judgment was to be "a memorial unto the children of Israel, that no stranger, which *is* not of the seed of Aaron, come near to offer incense before the LORD; that he be not as Korah, and as his company: as the LORD said to him by the hand of Moses" (Num. 16:40). "And of Levi he said, ... They shall teach Jacob thy judgments, and Israel thy law: they shall put incense before thee, and whole burnt sacrifice upon thine altar" (Deut. 33:8, 10). "The offering of incense was considered the most sacred and important part of the daily morning and evening services. These hours of worship, at each of which a lamb was offered (Exod. 29:38–42) for a burnt offering, were known as the morning and evening 'burnt offering,' or 'sacrifice' (2 Chron. 31:3; Ezra 9:4, 5), or as 'the time of incense' (Luke 1:10; see Exod. 30:7, 8)."[64]

When the men of Israel permitted, supported, and encouraged the women of Israel to get directly involved in the practice of the worship system and to adopt the exclusive priestly rites, it signaled their complete downfall. Through the influence of the women and their participation in that which the Lord had forbidden and ordained to be done solely by the priests from Aaron's line, Judah was doomed. As the clouds of unholy incense ascended over Judah and the women adopted strange gods, incorporating them into the decaying Jewish nation, creating a pluralistic worship system, the men descended deeper into apostasy and made their way back to Egypt to their final demise.

Strange that it was through a woman's desire to elevate herself that mankind was overcome in the beginning (Gen. 3:1–6). The fall of Israel, just prior to entering in the land of Canaan, was caused by heathen women. The record states: "And Israel abode in Shittim, and the people began to commit whoredom with the daughters of Moab. And they called the people unto the sacrifices of their gods: and the people did eat, and bowed down to their gods. And Israel joined himself unto Baalpeor: and the anger of the LORD was kindled against Israel" (Num. 25:1–3). The mightiest strongman in history—Samson—could overcome thousands of men, yet it only took one dissolute woman to cause his defeat (Judges 16:18–20). It was through a woman that David fell, he being the greatest king of Israel (2 Sam. 11:2–5). The wisdom of Solomon—and he was the wisest man that ever lived—was not sufficient to stand up against the subtlety of women (1 Kings 11:1–8). Moreover, the last book of the

---

64 *The Seventh-day Adventist Bible Commentary*, vol. 5, 1978, p. 672, commentary on Luke 1:9.

Bible reveals that the final takeover of the world in apostasy will again be through a woman—the Mother Church that has many daughters (Rev. 13–18). One can never underestimate the power of women—either for good or for evil.

The greatest blessings to the human race and the greatest debacle of men, as well as a plethora of evils have resulted when women, dissatisfied with their God-ordained roles, have meandered over into that which the Lord has not ordained.

16.

Christ and his Church

Marriage is frequently employed in Scripture as an illustration of the relationship between Christ and His people (see, for example, Isa. 54:5; 62:5; Jer. 3; Ezek. 16:8–63; Hosea 2:18–20; Eph. 5:25–32). The high priest, who typified Christ, was permitted to marry only a woman who was a pure virgin (Lev. 21:10–14). Christ compares himself to a husband, and the church to a wife.

When God used analogies or illustrations to show His intimate relationship with His church, He chose a woman, not a man. God said: "Now when I passed by thee, and looked upon thee, behold, thy time *was* the time of love; and I spread my skirt over thee, and covered thy nakedness: yea, I sware unto thee, and entered into a covenant with thee, saith the Lord GOD, and thou becamest mine" (Ezek. 16:8). This language is an allusion to Jerusalem's coming in contact with God when He rescued her out of Egypt and kept His eye on her until she "became of age." Then, He made a covenant with her. What did "spread my skirt over thee" mean? In those days, men wore tunics. When a male placed the bottom of his robe or tunic over a lady, it signified his intent to confer upon the maiden the honor of marriage. And it can also refer "to the Oriental custom in which a newly married man spreads a fold of his long, skirtlike outer robe over his wife, to signify that she is his property, and that he alone has power over her person (Ruth 3:9–14; 4:10; Eze. 16:8)."[65]

If you have noticed, the Lord is identifying Himself, in this illustration, as the husband to be. As He himself ordained, He is the one who, as the groom, initiates the betrothal. Then, as He casts His skirt over the woman, He makes her His own. From the start, He found and espoused her, then He married her, and she became dependent upon Him. It is He who swears by an oath and offers the covenant. He is the provider; He nourishes her; He is her protector and sustainer. He is the head!

---

65 *The Seventh-day Adventist Bible Commentary*, vol. 1, p. 1032, commentary on Deuteronomy 22:30.

Ezekiel 16:2–7 reveals, in allegorical language, the deplorable condition in which God found Jerusalem. Verses 9–14 speak of all that the Lord had done to make her glorious. In symbolic language describing a woman, He depicts Jerusalem's splendid sanctuary with its gold, silver, and rich embroideries. From an uneducated rabble, God built a glorious, organized nation. They became the envy of the other nations. As Jerusalem's husband, He provided the wherewithal to make the "daughter of Zion to a comely and delicate *woman*" (Jer. 6:2).

After all that He did for her, however, she became unfaithful. Then, portraying Himself as a distraught husband, the Lord revealed in Ezekiel 16:15–43 the gravity of Jerusalem's unfaithfulness and abandonment of their Husband. He describes her "as a wife that committeth adultery, *which* taketh strangers instead of her husband" (verse 32)! In spite of her betrayal, God tells her in love and mercy: "Nevertheless I will remember my covenant with thee in the days of thy youth, and I will establish unto thee an everlasting covenant" (verse 60).

In reference to God and His church's relationship, Paul wrote, "For I am jealous over you with godly jealousy: for I have espoused you to one husband, that I may present *you as* a chaste virgin to Christ" (2 Cor. 11:2). In this text, Paul is acting as the "best man" between the church and the Lord, which was the custom in those days. John the Baptist was also the "middleman," or, as we would call him today, "the best man," between Israel and Christ. The Baptist told the people: "He that hath the bride is the bridegroom: but the friend of the bridegroom, which standeth and heareth him, rejoiceth greatly because of the bridegroom's voice: this my joy therefore is fulfilled" (John 3:29). Later, referring to himself, Jesus said: "Can the children of the bridechamber fast, while the bridegroom is with them? as long as they have the bridegroom with them, they cannot fast. But the days will come, when the bridegroom shall be taken away from them, and then shall they fast in those days" (Mark 2:19, 20). There is no question that Jesus portrays Himself as the husband, and shows Himself as the head of His bride, the church. In turn, the church is shown as a dependent bride or wife relying upon Him to do all that is expected of the husband. By precept and example, God not only established an order but also ordained this headship with the intent that all who follow Him come into full harmony with it. He appeals to husbands to be loving and responsible and the head of the home; he appeals to the wife to be submissively true, loving, and supportive.

Biblically speaking, the church is a woman, and her husband is the man Christ. As Paul wrote, "I have espoused you to one husband" (2 Cor. 11:2). "For the husband is the head of the wife, even as Christ is the head of the church: and he is the saviour of the body. Therefore as the church is subject unto Christ, so *let* the wives *be* to their own husbands in every thing" (Eph. 5:23, 24).

To those desiring the office of a bishop, Paul wrote: "A bishop then must be blameless, the husband of one wife ... One that ruleth well his own house, having his children in subjection with all gravity; (For if a man know not how to rule his own house, how shall he take care of the church of God?)" (1 Tim. 3:2, 4, 5). A bishop or elder was to be the overseer of the churches. Concerning this, Paul wrote, "Let the elders that rule well be counted worthy of double honour, especially they who labour in the word and doctrine" (1 Tim. 5:15). "Remember them which have the rule over you, who have spoken unto you the word of God: whose faith follow, considering the end of *their* conversation" (Heb. 13:7). "Salute all them that have the rule over you, and all the saints" (Heb. 13:24). Therefore, if a woman is a pastor, she, by virtue of her position, would have to be the spiritual ruler over her husband, thus reversing the order established by God when He said to Eve: "thy desire *shall be* to thy husband, and he shall rule over thee" (Gen. 3:16). It is with this understanding that Paul was inspired to write: "Therefore as the church is subject unto Christ, so *let* the wives *be* to their own husbands in every thing" (Eph. 5:24). It is the man who is to rule over his household and over the churches. This was also to be the case with the deacon. "Let the deacons be the husbands of one wife, ruling their children and their own houses well" (1 Tim. 3:12).

This "ruling" was *not* to be a dictatorial rigorous overcharge. It came with a biblical qualification. "The God of Israel said, the Rock of Israel spake to me, He that ruleth over men *must be* just, ruling in the fear of God" (2 Sam. 23:3). As an example, Abraham is singled out: "For I know him, that he will command his children and his household after him, and they shall keep the way of the LORD, to do justice and judgment" (Gen. 18:19).

The union of a man and woman is the only natural relationship that comprises a scriptural marriage. Therefore, only a man can meet the required instinctive role of a pastor, which represents the man Christ.

Of all the issues that we have seen coming and going throughout our personal church journey, none has fueled so much passion and had such potential of causing schisms among believers as this women's issue. My wife and I have trained hundreds of women in soul winning and believe they play an important part in contributing to the spreading of the gospel. Nonetheless, the truth that women can aptly carry out the function of sharing the good news does not translate into transforming them into that which the Lord has not ordained. A woman can never be a father. Conversely, a man can never be a mother. These are basic truths. Yet, the profound simplicity of these facts urges a candid indictment of transgender ideology.

> *If a woman is a pastor, she, by virtue of her position, would have to be the spiritual ruler over her husband, thus reversing the order established by God.*

In the final analysis, though things have become convoluted, ecclesiastically speaking, God's church can and must return to its primitive godliness. It must untangle itself from the sophistry of the world. It must abandon the twists that have coerced it into confusion, and it must regain its proper relationship with her God. Men must become Christlike men, and women must return to their godlike standing—not as elders, but rather as mothers of Israel. Christ is coming soon to gather His church. He is expecting to gather the church clad in His righteousness, which is represented by the woman adorned with the sun and standing on the moon, a figure of the Old Testament. Crowned with twelve stars, a symbol of the twelve apostles of the New Testament, Christ's church must function within the confines of the Holy Scriptures, where men are men, and women are women. We must get back to God's ordained order!

May Christ's church repent of the abuses of women and provide ways in which women who have a burden for ministry (the function and not the role) can be provided opportunities to fulfill their heartfelt longings without violating God's ordained order.

Torres, an evangelist, soul-winning trainer, and church administrator, has provided a biblical study on the subject of ordination.

TEACH Services, Inc.
P U B L I S H I N G

We invite you to view the complete
selection of titles we publish at:
www.TEACHServices.com

We encourage you to write us
with your thoughts about this,
or any other book we publish at:
info@TEACHServices.com

TEACH Services' titles may be purchased in
bulk quantities for educational, fund-raising,
business, or promotional use.
bulksales@TEACHServices.com

Finally, if you are interested in seeing
your own book in print, please contact us at:
publishing@TEACHServices.com

We are happy to review your manuscript at no charge.

CPSIA information can be obtained
at www.ICGtesting.com
Printed in the USA
JSHW051140280522
26383JS00016B/173